Ending Cycles of Violence II
Kenyan Quaker Peacemaking Response to 2007 and 2013 Elections

Other Books from Madera Press:

David Zarembka, 2011. *A Peace of Africa: Reflections on Life in the Great Lakes Region.*

Joy Zarembka, 2007. *The Pigment of Your Imagination: Mixed Race Families in a Global Society.*

Other Books from Producciones de la Hamaca:

Sadie Vernon, 2000. *In Transit: The Story of a Journey.*

Mary R. Hopkins, 2009. Men of Peace: *World War II Conscientious Objectors.*

Judith Bender and Anneke Bender, 2011. *Explorations in Art: The Journey of a Mother and Daughter.*

Pamphlets for Quaker Institute for the Future (QIF):

Ed Dreby and Keith Helmuth, 2008. *Fueling Our Future: A Dialogue about Technology, Ethics, Public Policy, and Remedial Action.* QIF #1.

David Ciscel, Barbara Day, Keith Helmuth, Sandra Lewis, and Judy Lumb, 2011. *How on Earth Do We Live Now? Natural Capital, Deep Ecology, and the Commons.* QIF #2.

Anne Mitchell with Pinayur Rajagopal, Keith Helmuth, and Susan Holtz, 2011. *Genetically Modified Crops: Promises, Perils, and the Need for Public Policy.* QIF #3.

Leonard Joy, 2011. *How Does Societal Transformation Happen? Values Development, Collective Wisdom, and Decision Making for the Common Good.* QIF #4.

Ed Dreby, Keith Helmuth, and Margaret Mansfield, Editors, 2012. *It's the Economy, Friends: Understanding the Growth Dilemma.* QIF #5.

Ed Dreby and Judy Lumb, Editors, 2012. *Beyond the Growth Dilemma: Toward an Ecologically Integrated Economy.* QIF #6.

Ending Cycles of Violence II

Kenyan Quaker Peacemaking Response to 2007 and 2013 Elections

Judy Lumb, Kathy Ossmann, Joe Ossmann
and David Zarembka

Foreword by Joseph Mamai Makokha

Producciones de la Hamaca
Caye Caulker, Belize

Madera Press
Washington, D.C.

Producciones de la Hamaca is dedicated to:

—Celebration and documentation of Earth and all her inhabitants,
—Restoration and conservation of Earth's natural resources,
—Creative expression of the sacredness of Earth and Spirit.

Contents

Preface

Ending Cycles II is an updated version of *Ending Cycles of Violence: Kenyan Quaker Peacemaking Response to the 2007 Election* with the results of the 2013 election added. When I volunteered for the African Great Lakes Initiative (AGLI) in Kenya beginning in January 2012, David Zarembka assigned me the task of documenting the work of Friends in the violent aftermath of the Kenya 2007 election. In the peacemaking tradition of the Religious Society of Friends, Quakers initially provided humanitarian assistance to many internally displaced people, and then began a counselling and trauma healing effort that is still ongoing. For long-term peacemaking, Friends developed a peace curriculum for every educational level, from primary through secondary schools and for the training of pastors in the Friends Theological College.

To document all this work, I interviewed 34 people and quoted liberally from the transcripts of those interviews:

Getry Agizah	Joseph Mamai Makokha
Cornelius Ambiah	Moses Masika
Frederick Amwoka	Hezron Masitsa
Betty Atieno	Ann Mbugua
John Bulimo	John Muhanji
Simon Bulimo	Hanningtone Mucherah
Agatha Ganira	Moses Musonga
Eden Grace	Benter Obonyo
Irene Gulavi	Eunice Okwemba
David Irungu	Bernard Onjala
Josphat Lime Jiveti	Judith Ngoya
Oliver Kamave	Wambui Nguyo
Gladys Kamonya	Wesley Sasita
Kingsley Kijedu	Joseph Shamala
Churchill Kibisu	Donald Thomas
Malesi Kinaro	Wilson
Francis Kutima	Margaret Wanyonyi
	David Zarembka

This updated version of the 2012 book, *Ending Cycles of Violence*, was made possible because Kathy and Joe Ossmann volunteered for AGLI to assist David Zarembka with the monitoring of the 2013 election. They had two major assignments. They supported AGLI's training, call-in center and election monitoring work during the campaign and election period. After the election they carried out an assessment of the peacemaking work of AGLI/Friends Church Peace Team in the Mount Elgon area.

The new Chapter Nine, The 2013 Election written by David Zarembka, Kathy and Joe Ossmann, describes what happened in the much anticipated 2013 Kenya election. Beginning with civic education on the new constitution, this chapter describes the experience of election observers and citizen reporters. While the process appeared orderly and there was no repeat of the extensive violence that followed the 2007 election, many anomalies were documented.

The new Chapter Ten, Assessment of Friends' Peacemaking Work: Mount Elgon written by Kathy and Joe Ossmann, describes their work, along with Benter Obonyo and Ezra Kigondu. They interviewed 89 individuals in six Mt. Elgon communities, who had been participants in one or more of the Friends peacemaking programmes (see Appendix for interview methods and list of interviewees). The interviews took place the last week of March, just after the Kenyan national elections on March 4, 2013, which allowed exploration of the relationship between the Friends programmes and the contrasting levels of violence during the last two election periods.

Kenya has not only the most Quakers in the world, but a complex of interacting Quaker organizations that have all played their roles in this peacemaking work of Friends. A description of the various organizations and yearly meetings of Friends in Kenya is provided in the Appendix.

Judy Lumb
May 2013

Acknowledgements

I am very grateful to all of you that I interviewed, who shared so deeply of your experiences and your valiant efforts to end the cycles of election violence in Kenya. Thanks go out to Eden Grace for providing minutes, reports, and photographs that enrich this book, to Hezron Masitsa and David Zarembka for sharing their insight into Kenyan politics, and to Jean Smith for leading me to the history of the Alternatives to Violence Project (AVP). Those whom I interviewed, as well as Dorothy Beveridge, Claudia Huff, and Dawn Rubbert reviewed the manuscript. I am grateful for all your very helpful comments.

As I travelled in Kenya doing interviews, Eden Grace, Geeta Jyothi McGahey, Ann Riggs, and Douglas M'mbala Shikuunzi all housed and fed me. Thanks for your gracious hospitality! I am especially grateful to Gladys Kamonya and David Zarembka who welcomed me into their home for three months and took care of my every need with delicious food, warm friendship, and even a haircut. Thank you, one and all for a wonderful Kenya experience! I will be holding you all in the Light as you approach the next Kenya election.

Atlanta Friends Meeting, Kathy Johnson, Carolyn Manley, Dan and Sue May, Beatrice Petito, Bill Prince, Becky Schmitz, Bert and Karen Skellie, Judy Smedberg, Kathy Stoltz, Rolene Walker, and Pat Williams all contributed to my leading to go to Africa. Thank you for making this project possible!

Judy Lumb
March 21, 2012

We would like to express our deep gratitude to the Mt. Elgon residents who took the time and effort to meet with us and share their stories. We appreciate their honesty, courage, perceptive remarks, and useful suggestions. We are also grateful to all those on the mountain who offered hospitality in their homes, offices, shops, and churches. The children especially touched our hearts and made us feel like celebrities.

We could never have left square one without our Friends Church Peace Team (FCPT) support team. Getry Agizah,

FCPT Coordinator, and Peter Serete, FCPT Call-in Center Coordinator, were our ever ready safety net. They got us to and from our base in Chwele, handled lodging arrangements, arrived at strategic times to assist, and provided helmets for the inexperienced motorbike passengers from America. Many thanks; your efforts allowed us to just show up and do our work.

We are especially grateful to Pastor Erastus Chesondi, who gently guided and cared for us during our days on the mountain. He arranged for meals, transport, venues, people to interview, schedules that flowed flawlessly, and, managed to get us down the mountain before the rains hit each day. Every meal, every *bodaboda* (motorbike) ride up and down the mountain that he arranged revealed his care for us. When we arrived in each location his network of resource people were there helping with logistics of people and places. We could see why AGLI/FCPT coordinators refer to him as an effective mobilizer. It is the stuff of miracles that he is able to do so much after what he has been through. Although a pastor in the Maranatha Church, he is said to embody the Quaker peace testimony more effectively than many Quakers.

The whole assessment team is grateful to David and Gladys for providing space in which we could do our work together and to those who have conducted assessments for AGLI/FCPT before us. They provided helpful models, standards and ideas that made our process easier.

We are grateful to the African Great Lakes Initiative (AGLI) of the Friends Peace Teams (US) who provided funding and administrative support. Special thanks to all those in America who contributed to the extended service volunteer fund. Most fervent thanks to David Zarembka, AGLI Coordinator, who has guided the process from start to finish. We thank David and his wife Gladys Kamonya for opening their home to provide a home base during our three months in Kenya. The *chakula* (food) was great, the services very helpful, and the friendship without price.

Kathy and Joe Ossmann
May 28, 2013

Foreword to 2012 Edition

Reading *Ending Cycles of Violence: Kenyan Quaker Peacemaking Response after the 2007 Election*, my mind is rekindled on what I did and witnessed during the 2007/2008 post-election violence. It reminds me of that time when travelling was impossible. For almost two weeks communication with relatives and friends was totally cut off. In my own location, high in Mt. Elgon, a family of 12 members were slaughtered one after the other and thrown in one pit latrine. Very horrifying!

It required a lot of courage for one to plunge his or her life into the dangerous response to the violence, but that was exactly what Kenyan Quakers did! Western region, Nyanza, Rift Valley, Nairobi, Coast Region, name it: wherever Quakers were, their lives were exposed to the danger of death. Fortunately, none was harmed.

To write this book Judy Lumb had to travel to many places looking for whom to interview. She had to be patient listening to stories, sift through them, and come out with relevant messages worth publishing. A lot was accomplished by Kenyan Quakers under very threatening situations. Quakers the world over generously responded to the ugly situation in Kenya by raising funds for the work.

Completing this foreword without appreciating the involvement of David Zarembka would have been unfair. By assigning Judy to document Kenyan Quakers' response to 2007 post election violence during her stay in Kenya, David was answering my question to him: "how will the generations to come know what Quakers did in response to the 2007/2008 post-election violence?"

I am now relieved that there is a record to refer to now and in the future. May each reader have the full appetite to read the book to the last full stop.

Joseph Mamai Makokha
Chairman, Friends Church Peace Team
March 28, 2012

List of Abbreviations

AGLI	African Great Lakes Initiative
AFSC	American Friends Service Committee
AVP	Alternatives to Violence Project
CAPI	Change Agents for Peace International
FCPT	Friends Church Peace Team
FPCD	Friends in Peace and Community Development
FUM	Friends United Meeting
FWCC	Friends World Committee for Consultation
HROC	Healing and Rebuilding Our Communities
QPCC	Quaker Project on Community Conflict
QPN	Quaker Peace Network
QPSW	Quaker Peace and Social Witness
RPP	Reflecting on Peace Process
ToT	Training of Trainers
TTT	Turning the Tide

Raymond Ojiambo

Kakamega electronics shop burned

Raymond Ojiambo

Internally Displaced People (IDPs) At Chwele

CHAPTER ONE
Introduction

Nairobi—December 2007

Hanningtone Mucherah: "As the delay in announcement of the election results proceeded, tensions started rising in Kibera. I took the initiative to walk around. I saw people gathered around a radio. Then the Press Conference was over and all hell broke loose. Everything was wild. Stores were being looted. I took a *matatu* [mini-van] to Kenyatta Hospital and started walking to Kibera on Ngong Road. I saw an armoured vehicle full of security forces headed for Kibera. It was all smoke. I was walking under gunfire in the smoke. I could hear people dying on Ngong Road. The policemen on Ngong Road were shooting at anyone. I saw two school girls shot in front of me.

"I ducked into a garage and went under an old car. I stayed there for 30 minutes and then continued walking slowly on deserted side streets. It was an unfamiliar part of town for me.

"Finally I got home and life started up again, but we were holed up in the estate. There were no kiosks open, no shops, no supermarkets, nothing moving. The rail was already uprooted.

"After three days I went out again and I saw vandalism, property damage. There was no direct incitement from politicians. It was tribal, but also between Christians and Muslims, a silent arm of the violence. There had been conflict between those two groups for some time."

1

"What really shocked me was at a Requiem Mass for those who had died that was being held by ODM [Orange Democratic Movement] leaders. There were 28 caskets in the front of the place. About 30 minutes into the service, I noticed police were around the outside of the field and suddenly tear gas canisters were shot right into

the centre where the caskets were. Then the shooting started. The police killed four young people there. Everyone ran and the caskets were just left there unattended." (Hanningtone Mucherah, Programme Assistant, CAPI)

****

John Bulimo: "Odinga called for a prayer meeting for those who had been killed in the violence. I went smartly dressed. They didn't know who were the newly elected MPs, so they thought I was one of them and I was seated among the dignitaries who were with Odinga. In front of the crowd were coffins with the corpses of people who had been killed in the post-election violence. There were several speeches and then I noticed that the whole field was surrounded by police. When Odinga got up to speak, he started singing the national anthem and the police started shooting tear gas canisters. Everyone started running and jumping the fence. I saw youth with petrol that they poured on the Posta [post office] and lit it on fire." (John Bulimo, Friends Pastor and Clerk, Quaker Peace Network-East Africa)

Nairobi Friends Churches Affected by Violence

David Irungu: "There are four local Friends churches in the Kibera slum area. They are ever full of people from most of the tribes. People are always coming to this area looking for employment and many of them come to church. There is a Luo young man who plays the keyboard in church. Even Kikuyus come to church. Only the Nubians do not because they are Muslims.

"The Mashimoni Friends Church is on the border of the Luo, Kikuyu, and Luhya areas of Kibera. That church was burned when the shops nearby were burned. The Kikuyus had many small businesses in the area and were the ones providing the employment for the church members who lived there. So they lost their jobs and that affected their tithing.

"Zablon Malenge, the Clerk of Friends Church in Kenya was a victim of the violence. His wholesale book and stationary warehouse was burned. His house nearby was not burned, but he has it rented and is living elsewhere. Four years later he is still gone.

"For the people of Kibera, life is now much more expensive. They used to have small businesses, but now they have to depend on the church. They come to the yearly meeting and ask for help. The violence had a severe effect on everyone. Many of the old men in Kibera died because of it.

"The Toi Friends Church was burned, but now there is a new structure. In Kibera you do not put up permanent structures because no one has title to the land. Everyone is just a squatter. So you just buy structures, you don't buy the land. But this church is now doing quite well because it is a Friends Church and they bring peace. And there is diversity in this church." (David Irungu, Pastor for Friends Churches in the Kibera slum of Nairobi)

Cheptulu

Moses Musonga: "As soon as the results came, we heard there was trouble, burning of houses. Cheptulu where I live borders with the Rift Valley. In the nearby villages across the border, there are many Luhya people from here that have bought pieces of land there. We heard that Luhya houses in the Rift Valley were being burned by  the Nandi. People started running away. They escaped with whatever they could, their cattle and household goods. They came here to stay with families and friends.

"My sister's husband was caught when they were burning houses. The people had formed groups to remain vigilant to protect themselves and their houses. Whenever the Nandi young boys came to burn houses, they would restrain them. When my brother-in-law tried to stop them from burning houses, they shot him with five arrows in the chest and killed him instantly. He was with other people who ran away, but he was a bit old, 74 years old. He was a lay-leader of the local church of the Pentacostal Assemblies of God, so they organized a funeral service at his home in the midst of all the violence." (Moses Musonga, Former General Secretary, FWCC-Africa Section)

Naivasha

Betty Atieno: "I was in Mombasa because I was doing some AVP work in the prison there. I was to go home for Christmas, but only after I voted. I was excited to be able to vote. It was very important to me. And then I was to travel home to Nyanza. I am a single parent and my daughter was with my cousin in Nyanza. Immediately after the announcement, the violence erupted. I could see people running in the streets with placards saying, 'No Raila, no peace,' passing by my window.

"I could not travel. I was worried about my family and friends, but I could not get airtime for my cell phone and even when I had airtime, calls didn't go through. I was only watching what was happening on the news. My neighbours were mostly Kikuyu and Kamba, so their homes were closer and they had all left, so I was alone on the block. I stayed locked up in the house for two full weeks. I didn't try to go out to the shops because none were open. I had a little stock of food, so that pushed me forward.

"Then I got a call from Malesi Kinaro saying they were planning some workshops in Kisumu with the staff of the Centers for Disease Control. I was very grateful for that opportunity, but it pushed me towards travelling. In as much as I had watched horrible things happen, I said, 'God, I'm doing your work. Please get me to Kisumu.' I got a bus ticket and went.

"Before that time there had been no problems in Naivasha, but just as our bus arrived, Naivasha erupted. Our bus pulled off the road where there was no trouble to let off passengers. Then we got word that the buses coming behind ours were hijacked and people from specific ethnic backgrounds were maimed and killed.

"Thank God our bus continued and I arrived safely in Kisumu. If I had been on the bus following ours, I would not be here today. I count myself very lucky. We were almost caught.

"They heard about it in Kisumu and were calling me to see if I was safe. I arrived safely in Kisumu, but the usual spot the bus stopped was not safe, so the bus went on to find a safe place for us to alight. Then I got a *bodaboda* [motorcycle taxi] to the hotel where the training had already started.

"I was lucky to have that training then because I could talk about the trauma I had experienced in those two weeks. Those trainings in Kisumu with the staff at the Centers for Disease Control went on for a month during which we had some bad news. Two newly elected Members of Parliament (MPs) were assassinated. That caused a lot of confusion and we had to stop the workshops and debrief." (Betty Atieno, AVP Facilitator)

Kisumu

"Things seemed OK, so I went to the office. At 1:30 pm I heard a lot of noise, people running, fire, tear gas. The news was that the ODM MP from Eldoret had been killed. I tried to leave, but the soldier at the lift stopped me. I told him I was a Luhya from Kitale. He told me to go with my ID only, no purse, not even money. I put my phone,  money, and ID in a small paper bag and went out of the gate.

"Two men were standing in the veranda and told me, 'Come here. What tribe are you? Where are you going? Are you sure you are Luhya?' I convinced them and went on. At the Nakumat shop the police were all staring at me.

"I called my friend and she said to wait for her and we would go together. She and her husband came and we went up the street. Some women were saying, 'Kikuyu here.' Some police told us to carry leaves, so we got some leaves, a sign of peace.

"But then we saw some young men who said in Luo, 'We are not at peace. Drop the leaves and pick up stones.' I dropped the leaves, but didn't pick up any stones.

As we walked, people were calling, 'Wambui, Kibaki,' describing me as a Kikuyu to the people up ahead. There was a crowd, tear gas, stones being thrown toward the police.

"Suddenly I was surrounded by young men and I was alone. I heard shouts, asking in Luo what my tribe was. Then I saw the young man next to me lift his *panga* [machete] and I knew I was dead. I closed my eyes, but held my head high. I shouted in English, 'Oh God, I'm dead!' I heard my friend say, 'Oh, Reverend!' (She calls me "Reverend")

"Then someone took hold of my arm and said, 'What are you doing? She is not Kikuyu. She is Luhya.'

"I didn't know that man. He was my angel who saved my life. He said to me, 'Follow me. If you go straight you will not reach the junction.' He pulled me, like a baby, to a house. The man there said, 'Why are you bringing this Kikuyu to my house? Do you want my house to be burned?'

"My angel told him I was not Kikuyu, but Luhya. The man asked me to speak my language, but fear kept me from answering immediately. He kept asking me questions, "What is the tribe of your father? What is the tribe of your mother?' I knew the answers. My mother and father are both Bukusu Luhya from Bungoma. But the words wouldn't come out, so he said, 'See, she hesitates. She has only learned the Luhya language.'

"My friends had followed me to this house, too. The man gave us some sweet potatoes and some water. I tried to eat a little, but couldn't. Then he said, 'I am not comfortable. People saw her come in here, but I will show you a shortcut where you can go safely.' We used small roads and, thank God, I reached my house alive.

"I did not know that man and I still don't know the house. Every time I go that route I am reminded and I look, but I cannot recognize anything. I have never seen that man again, my angel who saved me." (Judith Ngoya, Friends Pastor and Friends United Meeting Administrator)

Kakamega

Wesley Sasita: "I live 12 km from Kakamega, but from my place I could see houses burning. I can still see those ruins. Near my place a boy was shot dead. He did not participate in this, but he was a *bodaboda* driver. He was going on his business. The security people told him to stop, but he was going on his own business, so he didn't stop and they shot him. That one annoyed the people in the area because here is an innocent boy who has been shot. He did not participate and he was killed. So, people wanted to know, where do the Administration Police come from?

"Schools and all businesses came to a standstill. Hospitals had no services because the people had run away. You could not get any commodity in the market. Shops were closed. There was no transport. I usually use a *matatu*, but I had to walk the 12 km home from Kakamega.

"Those of us who had been identified as church workers were least attacked. But anybody in administration was looked at with suspicion. And the police were feared. You did not want to talk to them, even if they just wanted information from you." (Wesley Sasita, General Secretary, Kakamega Yearly Meeting)

Mt. Elgon

Moses Masika: "My church on the slopes of Mt. Elgon, Chikai Monthly Meeting, became a refugee centre for about 200 Christians from Mt. Elgon who had been moved by force from their homes. We took their cattle onto our land to give them grass to eat. We began a programme of giving them food. Some of us hosted some Christians in our homes and we also took some of the children into our families because they had nowhere to stay. Their houses had been burned. That we did while I was still at home.

"When it was time for me to return to school at the Friends Theological College, it was a problem on the side of transport, travelling from Bungoma to Kakamega and then down to Kaimosi because Bungoma is Bukusu Luhya, which are PNU [Party for National Unity], as compared to Kakamega which is ODM [Orange Democratic Movement]. Vehicles coming from Bungoma to Kakamega and vehicles that stay at Kitale could not come to Kakamega or they would be burned because it would be assumed they carried PNUs coming to Kakamega. It was a difficulty, so I used a motorbike of my father's. I went to my elder brother's house and he came with me to Kaimosi." (Moses Masika, Friends Theological College Bookstore Manager)

Turbo

Ann Mbugua: "We are Kikuyus who were living in the Sugoi location of the Turbo District near Eldoret. We had been living with these Kalenjin people surrounding us. When the post-election violence started, I was at home with my family. We rushed to our neighbour who tried to protect us, but all was not well. We went to hide in the nearby bush and, unfortunately, they came and told us to move away from that place. They didn't want to see us again. We went to take refuge at a church. We stayed there about two days, until they came, very many of them. They wanted to kill us in that church. But the elders of the church told them to leave us alone, so the elders decided to escort us to the Turbo IDP camp where we stayed for five months. My family and I didn't go back to our place at Sugoi because we had that fear. We came to stay at Mwamba." (Ann Mbugua, AVP Facilitator)

Benter Obonyo: "I am a Luo, but my family had leased a house from a Kikuyu in Spring Park, which is an area of Lugari near Turbo. There were rumours that Raila was the one to win the election. Some of our Kikuyu neighbours said, 'do you think that Raila can win the election? It can't be; it can't be.' We just took it for granted; we never thought of anything bad happening.

"On Sunday, December 30th, we went to church as usual, but the turnout was so poor. Many people never turned up. In the evening our neighbour came from doing business in the market in Turbo five km away, and said that things were not good in Turbo. People had been chased away and people are just running. But my sister and I decided to just sleep in our house.

"The next morning a Kikuyu neighbour told us, 'You mean you slept in this house? You are really risking. Why are you sleeping in this house when the situation is the way it is? We don't want you people to be hurt, we want you to shift from this house. You have to shift.'

"So, we removed a bit of our items, just a very few, to the National Youth Service (NYS). We stayed in the NYS, which was just open ground. We had no tent; we were sleeping in an open place and it was very cold. Whatever you had in your pocket, that was what you had to survive. We did not have big money because my sister was working, but she would do the work and then get the money to buy food. We thought, 'Now what do we do?'

"We called our brother in Eldoret and he said, 'Just stick where you are because there is no way we can save you because things are so bad.'

"So we couldn't move; we couldn't go anywhere. We called some friends and told them we were at NYS. They felt sorry for us, but there was no way they could help us. They just brought us some greens. We were there for a period of one week with only those greens to eat.

"Then the people at the NYS said that place was not safe because it was near the road and the attackers could attack us easily. They decided we should go to the police station on the other end. People were shifting, and again it was a difficult moment. We had no money. To move some of our things, we would have to pay transport to carry the luggage that we had saved, just a few. People who had vehicles could just move. Finally we asked one of our neighbours, 'Please, can you help us? We don't have money and we can't carry these things to the police station because they are too heavy for us.'

"He said, 'I will pack all the things that belong to me first and then the few things that you have. I will help you.'

"When we went to the police station, there was nothing. It was just in a *shamba* [field] where the maize had been harvested. So, if you had a *panga* [machete], you could slash those maize stalks for that place to be good. We stayed there, but again there wasn't food. Some people had carried food and we could see them eating.

"After a few days the Red Cross came with tents, but there were no poles, so we cut sticks from the forest. They also brought some food, so we began to have hope. We had food and shelter. We went back to see our house and everything there was burned to ashes. So we stayed in the camp. We could go to the forest for firewood to cook." (Benter Obonyo, AVP Facilitator)

****

Eden Grace sent an article to Friends United Meeting entitled, "Heartbroken in Kenya" in early January of 2008:
"I don't have a brilliant analysis to offer you about what's happened in Kenya. But it feels to me that I'm holding together some very contradictory truths in my heart right

now. Kenya is a peace-loving country that is sinking into base and senseless violence. Kenya is a mature democracy (certainly by African standards) where politicians somehow believe they can get away with blatant rigging. Kenyans hold fiercely to their national values of unity and peace, yet they are suddenly aware of the deep divisions among them. Kenya is an economic "success story" where huge segments of the population have been excluded from the rewards of development. Kenya is 80 percent Christian, yet church-going people are now burning their neighbours' homes. For every story we hear about hatred and destruction, there are a hundred stories about kindness and courage which are not being told. All these things are true, and have been true all along. The election pulled the veil away. It unleashed a level of emotion that has surprised everyone. We, like everyone in Kenya right now, are confused and heartbroken." (Eden Grace FUM)

****

These are a few first-hand experiences of the violence in Kenya after the December 2007 election. To understand what happened, we need to consider the history of Kenya and the causes of election violence. How did so many different tribes come to live in this area that became the country of Kenya? What happened to the people who had lived here for centuries when the British came and took over the country? How did the Africans extract themselves from colonial rule to attain their independence? What form has their democracy taken that would lead to such terrible election violence? These questions are addressed in a brief history of Kenya and her cycles of election violence, the subjects of the next two chapters.

CHAPTER TWO
A Brief History of Kenya

Precolonial Kenya

As long as there have been human beings on earth, they have lived in what is now the East Africa country of Kenya. Early inhabitants were hunter-gatherers speaking a language like modern Khosian (click) languages.

When climate conditions were wet and conducive to agriculture 30,000 years ago, Kushite people moved south from the area of current-day Egypt, bringing agriculture, animal husbandry, and cultural development. Around 500 B.C. pastoral people moved south from what is now Sudan, speaking Nilotic languages like that spoken by the modern Kalenjin, Luo, Maasai, and Turkana people. Around the first century A.D., farmers came east from the Benue River area in West Africa speaking Bantu languages such as that of the modern Kamba, Kikuyu, Kisii, and Luhya people.

Also in the first century A.D., Arabs traders began arriving on the Indian Ocean coast, attracted by valuable resources such as ivory, cloves, and slaves. The African coastal people (Giriama and others) were ironworkers, farmers, hunters, and fishers. By the 10th century, the Arab traders had introduced Islam and established the independent Malindi, Mombasa, and Pate, city-states on the coast. For communication among the Arab traders and the Africans, the Swahili language developed as a Bantu language with many Arab words and is now, along with English, one of the two official languages of Kenya.

This brief review of precolonial human history in Kenya accounts for her great diversity in cultures and languages with 42 different ethnic groups in a population totalling 38.6 million in the 2009 census. The following table shows the ethnic

13

distribution among the 12 major tribes or groups of tribes as reported in that census. However, these data have been challenged, so they are only presented as an estimate.

Population of Kenya in 2009 Census

Ethnic Group	Population	Percent of Total
Kikuyu	6,622,576	17.16
Luhya	5,338,666	13.88
Kalenjin	4,967,328	12.87
Luo	4,044,440	10.48
Kamba	3,893,157	10.09
Kisii	2,205,669	6.18
Kenyan Somali	2,385,572	5.71
Mijikenda	1,960,574	5.08
Meru	1,658,108	4.30
Turkana	988,592	2.56
Maasai	841,622	2.18
Embu	324,092	0.84

Colonial Kenya

The first European contact was in 1498 when the Portuguese explorer Vasco da Gama arrived. The Portuguese vied with the Arabs for control of the Indian Ocean until 1730 when the Omani Arabs prevailed and the Portuguese withdrew completely. In 1839 Seyyid Said consolidated Omani power by establishing a capital on the island of Zanzibar, now a part of Tanzania, and governed the coast of East Africa, including the present-day Kenyan coast.

The British Navy was sent in the late 19th century to secure their interests in India and to abolish slave trade on the high seas. The Omani Arabs did not resist the British Navy but Germany had already claimed the coastal area as a protectorate. At the Berlin Conference of 1885 the two European powers agreed to divide the coast into the area that is now Kenya as a British protectorate and a German protectorate which is the current Tanzania mainland. In 1887 Seyyid Said gave the British East Africa Company a 50-year lease on his holdings on the mainland of present-day Kenya.

The British plan to use the indigenous people that occupied the mainland areas as labour on their plantations was thwarted by the serious resistance they encountered, which is documented by Maina wa Kinyatti in his book, *History of Resistance in Kenya: 1884–2002*. One by one the various tribes fought valiantly over years and sometimes decades, but eventually fell to the modern weaponry and inhumane brutality of the British forces. Maina quotes the British commander, Richard Meinertzhagen,

"[T]hough the war-drums were sounding throughout the nights we reached the villages. ... I gave orders that every living thing should be killed without mercy. Every soul was either shot or bayoneted. We burned all the huts and razed the banana plantations to the ground."

Rather than face total annihilation, each tribe eventually negotiated a separate surrender with the British, involving disarmament, acceptance of the presence of the British and their military bases, security for missionaries and other travellers, payment of colonial taxes, provision of labour, and loss or reduction of their lands.

The British had already explored the interior and claimed Uganda as a protectorate, so they needed access to the interior. They began building a railway in 1895 from Mombasa on the coast to Kisumu on Lake Victoria, which is near the Uganda border. The railway fulfilled a Nandi prophecy of a massive black fire-breathing snake weaving its way through their land, so for ten years they put up a strong resistance. None of the Africans would provide labour, so the British imported over 30,000 workers from India, many of whom stayed after the railway was completed in 1903.

In order to pay for the railroad, the area that became known as the "white highlands" was opened for British and other European colonialists who began to arrive in 1902. At that time the Kalenjin were on the western Rift Valley slopes, the Kikuyu were in the foothills of Mt. Kenya, the Luhya were in the area south of Mt. Elgon, the Luo were around Lake Victoria, and the Maasai were nomads in the Rift Valley. Along with other groups throughout Kenya, they were all living sustainably with large wild herds of animals. But the

British perceived this as empty land available for them to do with as they pleased.

To make room for the European colonists, the Kalenjin, Maasai, Kikuyu, and other groups were moved from their fertile homelands to small semi-arid or less fertile areas. The African groups were crowded into small reserve areas defined by ethnic group, creating or exacerbating ethnic identities and conflicts. This forced segregation "divide and conquer" strategy of the colonial authorities facilitated the development of stereotypes and xenophobia.

The British directed the missionaries of each Protestant denomination to a different ethnic group. This orderly development was so that the missionaries would not compete for the same converts. The missionaries translated the Bible into those local languages, all of which helped to isolate the ethnic groups from one another.

Three Friends Pastors from Cleveland, Ohio, arrived in 1902 and settled in Kaimosi in the Western Province. They worked among the Luhyas, a combination of several similar ethnic groups. Established a year later in 1903, the Kaimosi Primary School became the first formal school in Kenya. Kaimosi Hospital was opened in 1911.

The European settlers established large farms where they grew coffee and tea for export, but the Africans were not allowed to grow any crops for export. Some Africans remained on the land as squatters or were hired from the reserves as contract workers. The Legislative Council composed of only Europeans passed a series of oppressive ordinances establishing a Hut Tax in 1901 and then a Poll Tax in 1910, both of which amounted to forced labour as the Africans were required to work on the Europeans' farms to earn money because those taxes had to be paid in cash. The Masters and Servants Ordinance of 1906 established a copper identification pass called *"kipande"* that all African males were required to wear outside of their particular ethnic reserve. From 1918 to 1939 several Resident Native Labourers Ordinances were passed, which eliminated squatters' rights to land, each more oppressive than the one before.

Even the squatters on the European farms were segregated by ethnic group. In her book, *Unbowed: A Memoir*, the late Wangari Maathai, who received the Nobel Peace Prize in 2004, describes her experience as a child in the 1940s.

"On Mr. Neylan's farm, people from many communities worked, including Luos, Kipsigis [a Kalenjin tribe], and Kikuyus, who without the economic and labour system the British instituted would not have lived in proximity to each other. Each community kept to the category of jobs assigned to it. Kikuyus worked in the fields, Luos laboured around the homestead as domestic servants, and Kipsigis took care of the livestock and milking. The communities also lived separately, which of course was deliberate. It was probably the master's way of making sure that everybody kept to their roles and remained apart. You would see a Kikuyu village here, a Luo village there, and a Kipsigis town down there."

In addition to the early resistance to British domination, and the Nandi uprising over the railway, several other uprisings occurred, including the Giriama uprising in the coastal area in 1913-4, a women's revolt in Murang'a in 1947, and the Mau Mau uprising of the 1950s that led to Kenya's independence in 1963.

Independent Kenya

While the Kikuyu people were quite resistant to the British takeover of their land, they also were the most adaptable and integrated themselves into the colonial economic system, becoming shop owners and civil servants. The first political protest against British rule was by the Young Kikuyu Association in 1921 led by Harry Thuku. In 1944 Thuku started the multi-tribal Kenya African Study Union, which evolved into the Kenyan African Union (KAU). Pressure from this group resulted in the first African representative in the Kenya Legislative Council.

From 1952 to 1956 the Mau Mau uprising was directed against British rule and the European settlers. The African population was divided between the loyalists who supported the British rule, the *status quo*, and the nationalists supporting independence. It was a brutal struggle with extreme violence, torture, and atrocities on both sides. Severe intimidation centred around "oathing" in which Mau Mau, who were mostly Kikuyu, extracted oaths that people would oppose British colonial rule and work for a free and independent Kenya. But these traumatic experiences have never been resolved and still contribute to inter-ethnic hostilities, a culture of violence in Kenya. Mau Mau leaders, who were tried and jailed, including Jomo Kenyatta, were hailed as Kenyan heroes of the independence movement.

While the British eventually over-powered the Mau Mau uprising, they instituted measures that released the colonial stranglehold and eventually led to independence. For the first time, Africans were allowed to raise coffee for export. African representation in the Legislative Council was increased, but that was not enough. There was a cry for "one man, one vote."

An agreement was reached at First Lancaster House Conference in London in 1960 that gave Africans 33 legislative seats compared to 20 reserved for Europeans, Asians and Arabs. A new African party was formed, the Kenya African National Union (KANU). By the election in 1961 there was a split and a rival party, the Kenya African Democratic Union (KADU) was formed. A constitution was developed and KANU and KADU formed a coalition government in 1962. Open elections were held in 1963 with no quotas and Jomo Kenyatta, having been released from prison in 1961, became the first President, leading Kenya from 1963 until 1978.

Land Reform

Kenyatta's view of land reform was rather conservative. He said that "whoever wants to sell, those with money could buy." European farm owners who were too frightened to remain in Kenya sold their land at cheap prices, which was purchased in large parcels by the elite Africans (Kikuyu, Embu and Meru). Some formed cooperatives or land companies and sold land in small parcels to others. Most of those who could buy assumed large debts and then had a difficult time paying them back. And, there were still many landless people, including many Kikuyu veterans of the Mau Mau uprising. They were asking why did they fight if they could not have land to secure a reasonable livelihood?

With financial support from Britain, some large farms were purchased from their European owners and given to Africans in 20 - 30 acre plots. Some of these areas were set aside for pastoralist communities, but this was never implemented. Kikuyu and other groups that had moved into the white highlands to work on the European farms bought land, which caused hostility, not ancient tribal hatred, but modern resentment based upon economic inequities, especially access to land.

In the late 1980s and early 1990s, official land registration resulted in more resettlement and dispossession. The government was composed of mostly Kalenjins at that time and they took the opportunity to chase those out of power off the land they had occupied for 20 years or more, especially if they had no official land title. These land issues are still at the heart of much of the hostility in Kenya. At a January 2012 hearing of the Commission for Implementation of the Constitution, the Maasai requested compensation for more than a million acres that they have lost since 1900.

Centralization of Power

Another issue that has generated unrest in Kenya is the centralization of power. At independence there were two approaches to the structure of the new government. KANU, which was composed of the larger tribes, supported a government with all the power in the centralized government, while KADU, which was composed of the smaller tribes, supported a federal system with a balance of power between the central government and regional areas, like in the United States. At the Lancaster Conference in 1960, the federal system won the day, so the first constitution made provision for regional governments, as well as a central government. Kenyatta reluctantly agreed with the federal system for the sake of independence, but then starved the regional agencies until they were ineffective and easily dropped in favour of a more centralized system. Concern for the corruption that comes from centralization of power in a few hands was another factor in the call for constitutional reform.

One Party Politics

By 1964, a year after the first free election, the KADU had voluntarily disbanded and its members joined the dominant KANU. After a couple of years, a new party formed, the Kenya People's Union (KPU), which was led by Jaramogi Oginga Odinga, a Luo elder and former Vice President. The KPU criticized the slow progress of land reform and favoured alignment with the Soviet Union rather than the West. Tom Mboya was a Luo, a KANU member, and the favoured successor to Kenyatta as President. When Mboya was assassinated in 1969, hostilities between Luo and Kikuyu reached a boiling point and riots broke out. The KPU was banned and very oppressive measures were used against their members, making Kenya effectively a one-party nation.

When Kenyatta died in 1978, Vice President Daniel arap Moi, a Kalenjin, succeeded him. Moi continued suppression of any opposition outside or within the KANU. In June of 1982 a constitutional amendment was passed by the National Assembly, which made Kenya officially a one-party nation. Just two months later, August 1, 1982, some air force junior officers and students attempted to overthrow Moi. Although the attempt was quickly squashed by the army and police, it increased Moi's mistrust of Luos and Kikuyus who were said to have masterminded the coup, so he filled the government, especially law enforcement and security personnel, with Kalenjins. Evidence that people opposed to the Moi regime were tortured in the basement of the Nyayo House was presented in the Truth, Justice, and Reconciliation Commission hearings in early 2012. This history is still a source of systemic injustices and ethnic hostilities.

The late Wangari Maathai describes the Moi's regime crackdown on opposition in her book, *Unbowed: A Memoir:*

"The University of Nairobi became a centre of student resistance to the government's activities. Security forces clashed repeatedly with student demonstrators who called for more political freedom. In 1985, government forces killed at least twelve students, while two years later the government closed the university—as it was to do several times in the coming years—and arrested student leaders. As a way to keep their opponents divided and insecure, elements in the government also played different ethnic communities off one another."

The activists worked through a secret organization called "Mwakenya." Some people associated with this organization were arrested and held without trial. Koigi wa Wamwere is an example. He was elected as a Member of Parliament from Nakuru North in 1979 and then detained for being part of the coup, although he denied any involvement. He left Kenya when he was released from prison two years later, but each time he returned, he was detained again for some years until finally in 2002 he was elected to Parliament again.

Other activists left the country, including well known author Ngugi wa Thiong'o, who is now Distinguished Professor of Comparative Literature and English at the University of California at Irvine.

In the 1988 elections there were some choices of candidates, but instead of a ballot, a system of queuing (*mlolongo*) was used where voters lined up behind their favoured candidate. They were counted and then told to go home. When the results were announced later, some candidates with short lines were declared the winners, but there was no way to verify, which generated an outcry for change.

Moi maintained that multiparty politics would exacerbate inter-ethnic hostilities, but heroic Kenyans, including Masinde Muliro, Kenneth Matiba, Martin Shikuku, and Jaramogi Odinga led the "second liberation." They organized the first opposition political rally called *Saba Saba*, which means "seven seven" in Kiwahili, because it was held on the 7th of July, 1990. Even though it was banned, hundreds of thousands of people attended. Security forces broke it up, killing several people, but Moi was forced to end the one-party state. A constitutional amendment that allowed multiple parties was passed by the National Assembly in 1991. Thus began the cycles of election violence, which is the subject of the next chapter.

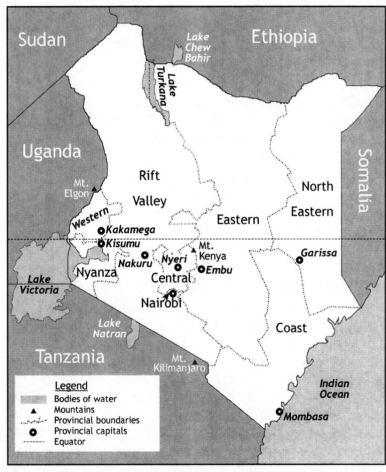

Map of Kenya showing the eight provinces and their provincial capitals as they were when the 2007 election occurred. Since then election reform has eliminated the provinces and created 47 counties.

Chapter Three
Cycles of Election Violence

1992 Election - Violence Before and After

In the lead-up to the multiparty election of 1992, a new party called the Forum for the Restoration of Democracy (FORD) was formed under Kikuyu, Luhya, and Luo leaders. But Kalenjin KANU political leaders, concerned that their hold on power would be diminished, scheduled public meetings in the Rift Valley and warned FORD leaders and Kenyans other than Maasai and Kalenjin to stay out of the Rift Valley. Violence broke out between Luo and Kalenjin on one former European settler farm where Luo had bought land that the Kalenjin thought was rightfully theirs. Violence is contagious and quickly spread to other areas in the Rift Valley where Kikuyu, Luhya, and Luo houses were burned.

Malesi Kinaro remembers it well: "In December 1991-1992 there were very terrible clashes. We were a one-party state and a serious dictatorship. A multiparty democracy was sweeping Africa, so obviously our civil society was very active. When the President realized these people were getting serious, he incited his people. We just woke up and we had no home. My brother-in-law was staying there. We were teaching in Kakamega. He said, 'Houses are burning everywhere. We don't know why. All the non-Kalenjin houses are burning.'"

By the time of the 1992 election, 1,500 people had been killed and 300,000 displaced, including a large number of children. Because of the control exerted by the strong centralized government, police, security forces, and courts acted for the attackers, helping to run the opposition forces out of the area. A parliamentary investigation was thwarted by the central government. Church leaders laid the blame clearly on the politicians for inciting the violence, but land conflicts dating from the colonial period and subsequent resettlement account for its quick spread.

The violence was curtailed in time for the election by increased security and enforced curfews. Moi won re-election with 37 percent of the vote because the opposition was split three ways between Mwai Kibaki of the Democratic Party, and two candidates from FORD, which split according to ethnic group, Oginga Odinga, a Luo, and Kenneth Matiba, a Kikuyu.

For a time after the election, Kenya was calm, but after all the international election monitors, journalists, and representatives of the World Bank and the International Monetary Fund left, the KANU youth group returned to their attempt to remove Kikuyu, Luhya, Luo, and Kisii from the Rift Valley. Those displaced from their homes were in camps. At the end of 1994 those still in the camps were taken by trucks with their meagre belongings across the ridge to the Central Province and left there with no attempt at resettlement.

President Moi filled his administration with fellow Kalenjins, but he also won the support of many of the elite Kikuyu businessmen who controlled the economy by protecting their business interests.

1997 Election - Violence Again

Before the 1997 election there was some violence in the Rift Valley, but the worst was in the Coast Province where Mijikenda were the original inhabitants. They formed militias and intimidated Kamba, Kikuyu, Luo, and Luhya residents who were told to go and vote in their own areas, even though many had lived in that area for generations. The violence lasted from the voter registration in June until November, before the December election.

As in the 1992 election, the opposition was split. Kibaki ran again under his Democratic Party; Raila Odinga, son of Oginga Odinga split from FORD and started the National Development Party. FORD had already divided into FORD-Kenya and FORD-Asili, so there were several opposition candidates. Moi won with 40 percent of the vote and Kibaki was second with 31 percent. Once the results were published, violence broke out again. Anticipating attacks, Kikuyu, Luhya and other groups that had been victims of election violence in the past formed vigilante groups, which exacerbated the problem as it only encouraged the previous perpetrators to more violence.

Joseph Mamai Makokha explained that "in 1997 Friends United Meeting came in with humanitarian assistance to IDPs and helped to rebuild houses that were burned. They helped everyone who was affected, not just Friends. There were no IDP camps then. The Friends went through the Chiefs who called meetings of the community and Friends spoke to them a Christian message of peace, but there was no programme like AVP then."

As this post-election violence was still simmering, 212 people were killed and over 4,000 wounded when a suicide bomber attacked the U.S. Embassy in Nairobi on August 7th, 1998.

By 2001, in the lead-up to the 2002 election, the Kikuyu vigilante groups, the sons of the Mau Mau, had developed a group called "Mungiki", which means "we are many." The Mungiki adopted an ideology that rejected Western trends and returned to traditional cultural values, including "oathing," which had been so divisive during the Mau Mau uprising. Their message was appealing to poorer Kikuyu who had been displaced by previous hostilities and, especially, unemployed young men. The Mungiki amassed power and wealth by intimidating and extracting bribes from the *matatus* (minibuses), which were mostly owned by other Kikuyus. The police made little attempt to control this activity and sometimes extracted their own tribute from the *matatu* drivers. Other groups were formed within other ethnicities to counter the Mungiki.

2002 Election—Free at Last, or Maybe Not

The multiparty constitutional reform included term limits for the President, so Moi was not eligible to run in 2002. Besides Mwai Kibaki and Raila Odinga, who had been opposition candidates in 1997, Uhuru Kenyatta, son of Jomo Kenyatta, and William Ruto, Member of Parliament from the Eldoret, were also contenders. Kenyatta became the KANU candidate with Moi's support. Learning from their previous losses due to divisions among the opposition candidates, Kibaki, Odinga, Ruto, and others struck a deal, forming the National Rainbow Coalition (NARC), composed of several parties. A new constitution was to be drafted that would include the post of Prime Minister, which would be held by Odinga, while Kibaki would be the President.

Kibaki won in a landslide with 65 percent of the vote and NARC parties won 58 percent of the seats in Parliament with many reformers elected, including the late Wangari Maathai. The country was euphoric with grand hopes for a balanced democracy.

But the Kibaki administration reneged on the deal made with Odinga and other supporters and, instead of maintaining an ethnically balanced government, replaced many of Moi's Kalenjins with Kikuyus, so the NARC coalition disintegrated. Kibaki was in a serious car accident, so he was sworn in with a cast on his leg. When Vice President Wamalwa Kijana died in London in 2003, the Kibaki government lost a key person.

The corruption that had characterized Moi's regime continued under Kibaki as the sources of these ill-gotten gains merely switched to support the new administration. In 2004 the media exposed some of this corruption, including the Goldenberg and Anglo Leasing scandals. The Goldenberg scheme, which went back to the 1990s, involved fraudulent export forms for gold and diamonds that did not exist and involved the Kenya banking system, even at its highest level. Excessive amounts of money were paid to Anglo Leasing for services and materials that were never delivered. Eighteen separate cases resulted from this scandal.

During the Moi administration, journalist John Githongo had revived a branch of Transparency International to investigate and document corruption at high levels, developing a relationship with the opposition, Kibaki's team. After the 2002 election he was tapped to be Kibaki's corruption czar. When he did his job too well, Githongo began to receive serious threats, so he resigned his post and fled to England with the information he had gathered. His story was published in the book *It's Our Turn to Eat* by fellow journalist Michaela Wrong.

Because the new constitution was drafted with much involvement from civil society, it included considerable reforms. But by the time it came to a referendum in 2005, so many of those reforms had been removed by the Kibaki government that many of those who were involved in its original drafting opposed the new constitution. The coalition that formed in opposition was led by Raila and called the "Orange Democratic Movement" (ODM). The ODM's "NO" campaign was successful in defeating the new constitution, which was a humiliating defeat for the Kibaki administration. Kibaki then reshuffled his cabinet, leaving out Raila and his supporters and further polarizing the two sides.

Periodic outbursts of violence plagued the country as there was no attempt to resolve lingering conflicts and historic resentments. For example, in January of 2005 a dispute in Turbi, a village in the north, led to the deaths of over 50 people, many of them children in a primary school.

In 2006 a scandal erupted after *The Standard* newspaper office was raided by armed men led by two Armenians. The office was ransacked, equipment stolen, and staff assaulted. Rumours circulated that the Armenians were hired to destroy evidence of corruption and involvement in drug trafficking by high government officials. The two Armenians were deported and six officials were suspended for their part in the raid, but the report of the investigation was never made public. It was said that NARC stood for "Nothing Actually Really Changed."

2007 Election - Violence

In 2007 Kenya's economy had improved along with the global economy and statistics showed that the proportion of the population in poverty had reduced, which gave the Kibaki campaign hope of winning re-election. However, the country remained very unequal, which generated much dissatisfaction. It is easy to identify the causes of violence as ethnic, but economic conditions clearly predominate, underscored by inequities based upon gender and region. And the violence is mostly associated with elections, indicating that these inequities and differences are exploited by politicians.

Kenya's rapid increase in population has resulted in a very young population. The role of the Mungiki is a good example. While they were mostly Kikuyu, they were not the elite that were part of the Kibaki government, but poor, unemployed, mostly young men with little hope of a better life. After a few arrests of Mungiki leaders early in the Kibaki administration, the Mungiki were tolerated and possibly even used for intimidation of those opposing government policies. But in the days before the election, amidst fears that the Mungiki might oppose Kibaki, police carried out a brutal crackdown in Nairobi and surrounding areas in which more than 500 young men were said to have been killed.

Kibaki gathered a coalition of parties into the Party for National Unity (PNU). The ODM formed the predominant opposition with Raila Odinga as their candidate for President. The campaign was marred by considerable violence, supporters of one party attacking those of the other.

On December 27th the election itself was fairly smooth and peaceful. Through Quaker organizations, Friends provided election observers. The Quaker Peace Network-Africa (QPN) coordinated 49 Kenyan and 29 international observers, including several associated with the African Great Lakes Initiative from Burundi, Congo, and Rwanda. QPN organizers were Hezron Masitsa in Nairobi and Rose Imbega in Kitale. Many of the leaders of the Friends Church in Kenya were election observers. The observers knew the vote totals of their polling stations, but when results were posted, only the totals from the larger constituency were posted, so the election observers could not check that the results that had been certified at their polling stations were recorded properly.

When the Electoral Commission of Kenya (ECK) announced the first results, they were from Odinga strongholds and showed him one million votes ahead, out of a predicted eight million total. That was a large enough lead that the newspapers called the election for Odinga in the morning editions on December 29th. But by afternoon the situation had reversed as the ECK began to announce results from areas where Kibaki was strong. ODM poll-watchers objected because there were reported irregularities from those areas, so the ECK delayed further announcements to investigate the charges overnight. In the afternoon of the 30th the ECK announced from a secure location that Kibaki had won by 231,861 votes. They immediately went to the nearby office of the Chief Justice for a private swearing-in ceremony. This was very suspect because normally the swearing-in ceremony would be a grand official occasion held sometime later with many national and international dignitaries present.

The ODM won 99 seats in the Parliament, while the PNU only got 45, one indication that the Presidential election was rigged. The ODM called for Kenyans to protest in organized civil disobedience, but police blocked sites for planned actions. Live radio and television were blocked, so peaceful protests were thwarted. Where protests did occur, they were broken up by police and army security forces using tear gas, water cannons, live bullets, and beating people with clubs.

Violence broke out immediately in the ODM stronghold areas of the country. Unresolved land disputes and resentments from previous election violence boiled to the surface again. Nairobi, Mombasa, and Kisumu were scenes of massive looting, especially targeting Kikuyu businesses. People were attacked, kicked out of their homes, and the houses were set on fire. On New Year's Day, 35 Kikuyu died in the village of Kiambaa when the Kenya Assemblies of God church was set on fire by Kalenjin warriors.

The violence died down only to be rekindled as Mungikis (Kikuyus) from Nairobi moved into the Rift Valley to retaliate against the Kalenjin warriors who were attacking Kikuyus. But then the Mungiki targeted Kalenjin, Luhya, and Luo residents of the area, instead of the perpetrators of violence.

Two of the newly elected ODM Members of Parliament were assassinated just over a month after the election. Melitus Mugabe Were was shot in front of his own house in Nairobi on January 29th and David Kimutai Too was shot in Eldoret on January 31st, 2008. Each of these announcements generated renewed violence.

In the first two months of 2008, over 1,133 (the official number) people were killed, thousands of women were raped, and property destruction was widespread. The violence resulted in more than 600,000 internally displaced persons (IDPs) living in police stations, churches, schools, and camps. Some estimates are even higher. That is nearly two percent of the population, one in 50, who were run out of their homes, most with just the clothes on their backs. They were told to go back where they came from, but most were from families who had moved to those areas in the colonial days to work on European farms, so had been there for several generations. They had nowhere to go back to.

This was the situation that Friends in Kenya faced as 2008 began. The rest of this book chronicles how they responded with wisdom, courage, and passion.

CHAPTER FOUR
Friends Response to Post-election Violence

Pastoral Letter

A few days after the post-election violence began, the Quaker Peace and Justice Committee of Nairobi Yearly Meeting met to see what Friends (Quakers) could do. Midikira Churchill Kibisu was the chair of that committee. He describes how the Pastoral Letter was written:

"The pastoral letter was written because we looked at what was happening in this country and saw the need for a response to the post-election violence from a Christian perspective, and especially a Quaker perspective since we are a peace church. The Quaker Peace and Justice Committee of Nairobi Yearly Meeting came together and sat nearly a full week. There were many aspects to consider. We had to weigh each statement as to what effect it might cause. We consulted Quakers in other areas of the country to get their views of how we should approach the whole matter."

The following pastoral letter was written on behalf of the Friends Church in Kenya and addressed to the Leaders of the Nation:

8 January 2008

Receive Greetings in the Name of Christ Jesus.

"You are my Friends if you do what I command you." (*John* 15:14)
"Righteousness exalts a nation, but sin is a disgrace to any people." (*Proverbs* 14: 34)

At this time of pain, horror, sorrow, suffering, insecurity in our beloved country, we as Friends Church in Kenya, being a PEACE church, are deeply concerned for the safety of ALL Kenyans and friends visiting Kenya during this time of Political

31

and Social Instability. May we start by referring to our Quaker values which have guided us over the past four centuries?

Quaker Peace Testimony

"We actively oppose all that leads to violence among people and nations, ... Refusal to fight with weapons is not surrender. We are not passive when threatened by the greedy, the cruel, the tyrant, and the unjust. We will struggle to remove the causes of impasse and confrontation by every means of nonviolent resistance available. We must start with our own Hearts and Minds. Together, let us reject the clamour of fear and listen to the whisperings of hope."

Our Principle is, and our practices have always been: "to follow after righteousness and the knowledge of God, seeking the Good and welfare of humanity and doing that which tends to the peace of all."

As Friends Church, our Goal is to have a Peaceful Society anchored in and as a consequence of the process of Truth, Righteousness and Justice (*Psalms* 89:14).

Our basic Principles and Values that under-gird our concerns compel us to make this call to you, our political leaders. These include:

Truth

Truth is critical to the establishment of legitimacy for the political class, that is, presidency and the opposition, if they are to enjoy the loyalty and respect of all Kenyans. This can only be achieved if the objective truth is that the Elections were "Free, Fair and Transparent". For us, "the Spirit of Christ, which leads us into all TRUTH, will never move us to Fight and War against any person with outward weapons, neither for the Kingdom of Christ nor for the kingdoms of this world". (*Luke* 22:49-51), (*2nd Corinthians* 10:4)

Peace and Justice

Kenyans are sad, angry and disillusioned today. We call on all parties to look back to 30th December 2002, when all Kenyans collectively celebrated the "hope" of a united democratic and prosperous society.

We call on all people "to object to everything which leads in the direction of war, preparation for it or supporting it! Our faith challenges us as to whether we are now ourselves to become a divided people, swept along by the streams of mistrust and fear, arrogance and hatred which produce tensions in the world; or whether by our own decision, confidence, and courage, we can become a bridge linking those elements which promote truth, justice and peace."

This battle is not about ethnicity per se, rather it is about economic injustice, and the youth across the board bear the brunt of it. There is an icy gap between them and the older age. There was hope and expectation that this nation would be steered towards a more democratic, united, just and prosperous society, where development would be experienced by ALL hardworking Kenyans. That hope was rekindled, with their participation in the just ended elections and the youth in particular saw the possibility of moving forward for the betterment of their lives. They feel cheated. They are expressing anger that the rich are getting richer, while the majority are living on less than one dollar a day. "A hungry person is an angry person". Justice is what they long for.

Simplicity

Quakers believe in modesty, serving humanity in love and harmony. In Kenya, there are gross inequalities in terms of sharing the scarce opportunities and resources. The rich are "Very Rich", while the Poor are "Very Poor" and the gap is widening. From the looting that has been witnessed across the board, it's clear that the present up-rising is not per-se ethnic, but rather, to a greater extent, "a Class-Struggle". "Money bags" "Rich-ness". "Quick money-making" e.g. pyramid schemes, have been glorified. The affluent conspicuous consumption and obnoxious display of wealth of the upper class, in a sea of poverty, have not helped.

The hopes and opportunities for the poor (have-nots) for upward mobility have been frustrated by continuing "joblessness" and false promises by politicians. The underlying perceived injustices of our economic disparities must be urgently addressed. A genuine honest and sustainable commitment to redressing the imbalances should be made. Otherwise we warn that the class "battles" will continue in one form or other. The youth are desperate, angry and impatient. The ordinary Kenyan does not feel or see the effect of the purported 6.5% annual growth of the economy or the benefits of the foreign investors.

The unsatisfactory manner in which corruption cases (Anglo-leasing/Goldenberg scandals) have been handled are seen as unjust and discriminatory against the poor who get heavy sentences for petty theft, yet the greedy rich go scot-free. This impunity, lack of accountability and arrogance of the corrupt rich, has fostered a deep-rooted anger that has exploded and must be addressed meaningfully, openly and fairly.

Life is Sacred. "Stop the Bloodshed"

As Quakers we value every person. We believe that "there is that of God in every person". Our central faith requires that we should proclaim, in deed as well as in word that war "is contrary to the Spirit of God, whose name is Love. The same spirit must animate our business and social relations and make us eager to remove oppression and injustice in every form."

As such, we renounce these senseless killings and urge the government, to take responsibility and restrain the security forces from using violent means of handling the "demonstrators". We urge all parties to give a listening ear to the people. Through their violence they are communicating a serious message. Please listen respectfully.

- Politicians should avoid using youths in their schemes to create mayhem in society.
- Supporters should stop being misused and abused by politicians.
- Party leaders must restrain their supporters from engaging in unlawful acts but should engage in peace building.
- The older people should be encouraged to counsel and dissuade the youth from violence.

Faith-based institutions should continue sending clear non-partisan, noninflammatory messages that resonate the life affirming, faith-filled, truth and justice-guided, peace-building, comfort-giving, reconciliation-oriented, repentance-seeking, confession-based messages of their faith.

[The pastoral letter continued with suggestions for solution to the crisis, which are superseded by the Grand Coalition that was eventually formed. The following activities were suggested:]

- Peaceful rallies must be allowed and organized to facilitate the healing process.
- Civil society and religious organizations should have forums to enhance reconciliation through dialogue, counselling and conflict resolution.
- Losers of Parliamentary elections on both sides and former ministers should desist from giving inflammatory statements motivated by their personal vested interests.
- All God fearing people should acknowledge and repent their sins (such as bribery, false witness, murder, rape, pride, arrogance, dishonesty and others) of commission and omission.

"If my people, who are called by my name, will humble themselves and pray and seek my face and turn from their wicked ways, then will I hear from Heaven and will forgive their sins and heal their land." (*2nd Chronicles* 7:14).

All presidential candidates have affirmed the need for a new constitution. We Kenyans are in dire need of a new God-centred and people-based constitution. All constitutional institutions have failed us: the presidency, parliament, ECK, Anti Corruption, Political Parties, Civil Society, Civil Service, Constitutional Commissions and especially the Ministry of Justice and Constitutional Affairs. The only institution that is still functioning faithfully is the people: they voted peacefully and in earnest, now they are in disarray because the existing constitution does not address the people's needs.

In conclusion, we as a Peace Church are committed to the process of national healing. Already we have institutions and programmes in place such as: Alternatives to Violence Program (AVP); Trauma Healing; Change Agents for Peace International (CAPI); the Quaker Peace Network, all with the necessary skills, knowledge and experience to help bring about healing and transform relationships.

We call upon the wider Body of Christ and other faith-based institutions to share in the restoration of a healthy, peaceful and just Society. God bless Kenya.

Midikira Churchill Kibisu,
Presiding Clerk of Nairobi Yearly Meeting

"The Pastoral letter was delivered to the two principles, Kibaki and Odinga, and to those attempting to negotiate a solution. We even sent it to Kofi Annan and we are told by those who were there that many of the suggestions that we made were used by that committee." (Churchill Kibisu)

Kenyan National Quaker Peace Conference

In 2008 Kenya had 15 of the 28 yearly meetings of Friends that belonged to Friends United Meeting (FUM). In recent years the January quarterly meeting of the FUM Board has been held in Kenya, so in the midst of the violence, the Presiding Clerk and General Secretary of FUM already had their tickets to come to Kenya and a venue had been booked for that Board meeting. They were advised not to make the trip.

Eden Grace explains how the Kenya National Quaker Peace Conference happened: "We decided to use the venue already booked and have a Kenya National Quaker Peace Conference of all Quaker leaders, representatives from Yearly Meetings and from NGOs (non-governmental organizations). Speaking personally, I had two objectives for the conference:

1) To revitalize the Peace Testimony among Kenyan Quakers. It is at the heart of the gospel, the core of our faith. The church bears this testimony.

2) To get the Yearly Meetings and NGOs working together. I believe that transformative work arises out of the worshipping body.

"The NGOs needed to ground themselves and the churches needed to revitalize peace work.

"The first step was to call together the senior level national church leaders and that meeting happened on the 14th of January. We brought to that meeting a proposal for a national conference. The proposal was endorsed by that meeting and the invitations went out from the FUM office.

"We sent out a Press Release announcing the meeting to the international Quaker media, a fund-raising effort to support the conference. *The Friend* covered it and AFSC's publication *Peacework*, did a big spread on it. I did an interview on Public Radio International on their programme *The World*." (Eden Grace)

From the 24th through the 27th of January 2008, 65 leaders in the Friends Churches of Kenya and a few international Friends met at Sheywe Guest House in Kakamega to consider what Friends could do about the ongoing post-election violence. Henry Mukwanja, Friends Representative to the

National Council of Churches of Kenya, gave an insightful overview of the root causes of the violence. He challenged the group:

"The church can influence the ODM and PNU to soften their hard-line stands that risk the future of this country. Irrespective of tribal identity, perceived or real, the church should be bold enough to encourage the main protagonists, President Kibaki and Hon. Raila Odinga to meet face to face and engage in serious honest discussions that will steer the country out of this crisis.

"The church should lead the society by example. As a church and nation, we need each other, whether Christian, Muslim, Digo or Luhya, ODM or PNU, we all need each other. The healing and restoration process of lost relationships should be enhanced. Trauma counselling of the IDPs and the perpetrators should be carried out in forums." (Henry Mukwanja)

Eden Grace wrote an article about the Conference, with summaries of two talks. Oliver Kisaka, a Friend and Deputy General Secretary of the National Council of Churches of Kenya, spoke on "Setting the context: What happened in the post-election period, what is the preliminary analysis of root causes, and how do we put it in a Christian framework?" He noted that "the spiritual life of Kenyans is too compartmentalized, too divorced from economic and civic engagement. He praised Friends for gathering in this conference to ask what is our responsibility, and encouraged us that "the Quaker light should shine!" He reflected that Friends have strengths to offer at this time. Our Testimonies are our strength to guide us. We have strong capacities in nonviolence training, and we should broaden these to look also at training for business and entrepreneurial participation. Finally, he challenged Friends to engage in advocacy on behalf of those who are suffering and oppressed."

Mary Lord, recently-retired Assistant General Secretary for Peace and Conflict Resolution at American Friends Service Committee, happened to be visiting Kenya at the time. She spoke on "The Peace Testimony: Biblical Basis and Practical Application." Eden Grace wrote of that talk:

"Implied in the affirmation of Peace as a matter of faith is the realization that it is not by our own power or knowledge that we make peace. It is the power of the love of God, of Jesus, of the Holy Spirit. Mary stated that if we do not begin from faith, our peace work will not be effective. If we do begin from a life-changing faith, then we have no other option but to be peace-makers.

"In living this Testimony over more than 300 years, Mary said that Friends have become 'researchers' of peace, experimenting and finding effective ways to witness in various contexts. She then gave several examples of ways Friends have given expression to the Peace Testimony.

"During the 20th century wars in Europe, Friends provided humanitarian relief to victims on all sides of the conflicts, a move that was highly controversial at the time. Mary remarked on the fact that the Friends most directly involved in this work felt that their efforts were inadequate, and struggled with fatigue and despair, but that the world community recognized their work by awarding them the Nobel Peace Prize in 1947. Their seemingly inadequate effort became a beacon to others about the way to make peace.

"Mary mentioned instances in which Friends have served as mediators and negotiators. She shared how Friends have established safe-havens for dialogue in the midst of violent contexts, and have offered leadership to various movements for social justice. Friends have increasingly been taking the role of supporting and training, and of lifting up voices and truths which need to be heard in the public discourse. Mary closed by remarking that, although we often despair that we are not making a difference, the reality is that the world is a more peaceful place because of the work of Friends.

"In the discussion which followed, Friends used Mary's historical examples as a way of approaching the current crisis

cont'd p. 42

Open Letter to the Leaders and Citizens of Kenya

The Quaker leadership of Kenya gathered together in Sheywe Guest House in Kakamega between 24th and 27th January 2008. The Friends Church in Kenya and Friends around the world are concerned with what has befallen Kenya in the last one month. As a peace church, we are horrified by the continued wanton destruction of human life and property.

Kenyans need to learn that any violent action they take against their neighbours is an act against God's way. Our actions and thoughts therefore must be rooted in the Gospel of Jesus Christ. In our last communiqué to the leaders, we implored upon them to uphold the principles of truth, justice, peace, simplicity and humility (*Psalms* 85:10) and to forgive each other.

We cannot be blind to what is happening to this country and its citizens. During the deliberations and reflections, representatives of the Friends Church realized that the underlying causes of the current conflict have been present since long before the general elections of December 2007. We note in particular: economic injustices, youth disempowerment and frustration, and cleavages of religion, ethnicity, class, gender and age.

To our leaders:

We thank our leaders for starting a process of negotiation, and we believe and trust that they will follow up in earnest with a negotiated settlement. In this context therefore we say to our leaders:

- We do understand your anguish at this time, and we ask you to approach the situation prayerfully. We urge you to relax your "hard line" political demands and dialogue more deeply for the benefit of the country, that no segment of Kenyan society emerges as "losers" but we all may "win" in a peaceful society.
- We urge you to reopen schools that have not opened, in order to allow students to continue with their education.
- We urge the leaders and elders of various communities not to incite or manipulate their youths to perpetuate terror among the citizenry, but to encourage and guide them to act responsibly.
- We denounce the instances of excessive force used by the police against the citizens.

To our fellow Kenyans:

- We appreciate the courage and passion that you, our fellow Kenyans, have shown since the beginning of the post-election violence by contributing and supporting the victims of violence, and we urge you all to continue with the same spirit.

- We appeal to you to engage in reconciliation among and rehabilitation of displaced people, integrating them back into the places from which they were displaced, not sending them to other parts of the country.

- We remind you that this country and its land belongs to all of us. Let us not destroy it for by doing so, we put our own future generations in jeopardy. We need a negotiated social contract to live together as Kenyans.

- We urge you to resolve problems in a peaceful way, because we know that there is hope for peace in this country.

- We warn you to desist from rumour-mongering which increases hostility and uncertainty, and urge you to use modern means of communication for positive ends.

- We know that those most affected by this conflict and violence are women, children, disabled and the aged. We must address their suffering, and protect and care for them.

- We encourage every Kenyan to look for "that of God" in every person and to treat life as sacred.

- As Kenyans, we urge you to uphold our core national values, practice forgiveness and embrace reconciliation.

To our fellow Christians and other religious groups:

- As people of faith, we must not engage in violence and revenge because if we do so we betray our faith in God.

- We invite you to join us in praying for deliverance from evil spirits which are at work in our country, and continue to intercede for Kenya.

As a peace church, we are involved in humanitarian, spiritual and social/economic empowerment of our people. We urge everyone to take time to assist his/her neighbour in order to bring normalcy to the affected people, affirming truth, justice, peace and reconciliation in our nation.

Jacob Neyole
Presiding Clerk, Friends Church in Kenya

Wesley Sasita and Gladys Kang'ahi at the Peace Conference

John Lumuria and Getry Agizah participating in the Peace Conference in Kenya. Participants spoke of reaching out to the youth, offering meaningful activities to counteract the temptation to violence. They spoke of reintegration of displaced people, and of creating centres for dialogue without fear. They urged Friends to take action "on the ground" and to persist in prayer that the power of Jesus may overcome the 'demons' of violence in Kenya right now."

A Plan of Action was agreed upon, which included immediate crisis-intervention measures and longer-term work. Resources were identified to support the work, both Kenyan and international, and procedures agreed on for managing the finances. The group appointed a Coordinating Committee of 13 members with seven *ex-officio* members representing Quaker organizations to carry out the Plan of Action described below.

Immediate Crisis-intervention Measures

To address the political crisis, the participating Friends decided to issue a public statement from this Conference, (*pages 39-40*) use the media to publicize messages of peace and reconciliation, document and disseminate stories of people acting in courageous nonviolent ways, engage in nonviolent direct action to stop violence and retaliation in our communities, and preach the gospel of peace, educating our own people on the teachings of our church.

To address the urgent humanitarian crisis, they planned to help the internally displaced persons (IDPs) with shelter, food, water, fuel, clothing, medication, first aid, health care, sanitation, trauma counselling, Bibles, activities, games, and access to schooling. They hoped to be able to mediate in situations of inter-community conflict, to assist in reconciliation between the IDPs and those who threatened them, so the IDPs could be reintegrated into the community and rebuild trust between neighbours. They understood that this would require crisis-intervention and trauma counselling. They hoped to scale up AVP to reach as many places as possible and establish listening programmes for people to tell their stories in a safe environment. To reach the children, primary

(*from left*) Lydia Bakasa, Henry Mukwanja, Rose Imbega, and Peter Shale at a tea break during the 2008 Quaker Peace Conference

(*from left*) Dorothy Selebwa, Nora Musundi, and Irene Gulavi also having tea at the 2008 Quaker Peace Conference

Coordinating Committee:

Getry Agizah	Joseph Mamai Makokha
Henry Apencha	Hezron Masitsa
Lydia Bakasa	Henry Mkutu
Seth Chayuga	Henry Mukwanja
Rose Imbega	Wesley Harun Sasita
Eric Lijoodi	Chrispinus Sifuna
	David Zarembka

Ex officio:

John Muhanji	FUM Africa Ministries Director
Eden Grace	FUM International representative
Gladys Kang'ahi	Clerk, FWCC Africa Section
Dorothy Selebwa	Clerk, USFW Kenya
Jacob Neyole	Clerk, Friends Church in Kenya
Moses Musonga	FWCC Africa Section, Executive Secretary
Sammy Akifuma	Clerk, QuakerMen Kenya

Eden Grace

Kenyan Quaker Peace Conference—27 January 2008

school teachers would have to be trained on the effects of trauma on young children.

To address the crisis of youth, the *bodaboda* (motorcycle taxis) drivers and other disaffected youth needed to be reached. There was a plan to organize youth work camps to help with humanitarian work and rebuilding, and to begin a pilot programme for civic and peace education in Quaker schools.

Possible cluster areas for longer-term work, and potential activities

A number of long-term activities were suggested to address youth empowerment, economic development, peace, justice and nonviolence, and the development of a culture of peace in Kenya. It was suggested that an organization be established that could organize the Friends' voice on public policy matters. Mechanisms were suggested for the spiritual development of the peace testimony.

Resources

The group assessed their resources. Friends United Meeting and Friends World Committee for Consultation were both active in raising overseas funds for relief and reconstruction. The Conference urged all Kenyans to raise local funds and to deposit them in the account of Friends United Meeting at the Kisumu Branch of Barclays Bank. They committed themselves that all money will be used efficiently and effectively, with transparency and integrity.

Donations from Kenyan Friends

Kenyan Friends were very generous in their donations of food and clothes for the internally displaced persons. Special collections were taken in Friends churches and all Yearly Meetings participated in the International Day of Peace.

Response from International Friends

Messages of support were gratefully received from international Friends. Financial support poured in from Friends all over the world. The African Great Lakes Initiative, Friends United Meeting, and Friends World Committee for Consultation all received donations for the Kenya relief work. Altogether approximately $350,000 was received, mostly in the first three months of the crisis, which allowed substantial humanitarian relief and then supported trauma healing and counselling work, which is ongoing.

Friends Church Peace Team

When the Coordinating Committee appointed by the Kenyan National Quaker Peace Conference first met, they decided upon the name, Friends Church Peace Team, and named officers for the group: Joseph Mamai Makokha, Chair; Rose Imbega, Vice Chair; Getry Agizah, Secretary; Chrispinus Sifuna, Vice Secretary; and Eden Grace, Treasurer. Later they designed a logo, a dove flying in front of the map of Kenya, which is shown at the beginning of each chapter in this book. They immediately got to work distributing humanitarian aid, which is the subject of the next chapter.

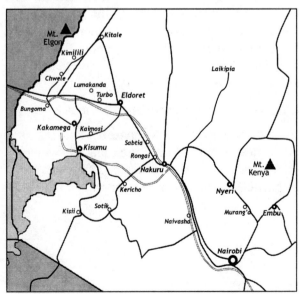

CHAPTER FIVE
Friends Humanitarian Assistance

While Kenyan Friends met all together at the Kenyan National Quaker Peace Conference, the work was necessarily divided into geographic areas. Most of those locations are shown on the map at the left.

Immediately after the election, travel was difficult, if not impossible, so Friends began working as they could wherever they were. Friends in Peace and Community Development (FPCD) worked first in western Kenya where most of the Friends Churches are, and then in Nairobi. Friends Church Peace Team (FCPT) worked in western Kenya. Because they are a days' journey to the east, Nairobi Friends worked independently to provide humanitarian assistance in the city and nearby areas of the Rift Valley. (*See Appendix for descriptions of Friends organizations*)

Kakamega

FCPD was quick to respond with humanitarian assistance in Kakamega. Malesi Kinaro describes the scene in Kakamega:

"The elections were very peaceful; the counting was very peaceful, at least most of it. But then came the announcement the President had won and the country went mad. We gathered three of us, members of FCPD. We had been talking peace to everybody else. Now is our time, what do we do?

"We went to town and found the Kikuyus at the Police Station, so many! So it was real—it has really reached here! We were hearing houses were being burned. We went in, just looking around, talking to people. Here were kids, just lying sleeping on the grass, just outside, nothing, all the elements. And our compassion was raised.

"The African Great Lakes Initiative (AGLI) had been funding FCPD for Alternatives to Violence (AVP) workshops. AGLI Coordinator David Zarembka was stranded in Vihiga with his wife Gladys Kamonya's family. We told him we wanted to take a little of the AVP programme money to just give the basics to these people and he said it was OK, so we made a plan.

"At that time the Red Cross had not come, nobody had come. We took them some kilos of sugar and rice, some greens, saying this was mainly for the children. There was one toilet for all those people and it was already full. We called on the Kakamega Friends Church, and the youth came and dug four latrines by the police station. We put up partitions to make compartments. We sat with them and tried to hear their stories. People were just in a state, but I had experienced it myself, so I wasn't expecting any serious talking. We continued going there.

"In the first week of the year we called the youth who were really mad, the ones who were causing all the trouble, to our office at the Uzima Foundation in Kakamega, which works with youth. They were so angry! They talked and talked and talked. The second day only half came back, but at least now their talking was more directional, more quiet. We asked if this was helping. They said,

"'No, it isn't helping. We don't even have customers. We usually have customers with the bicycles. Now we are going home with nothing. What can we do?' But I believe that really helped calm the situation in Kakamega, just talking, listening, and thinking of the best way forward. How can we slow this thing down?" (Malesi Kinaro, FPCD Director)

Centers for Disease Control

The U.S. Centers for Disease Control has laboratories in Kisumu and Nairobi with a few staff from the U.S., but a large Kenyan staff composed of various ethnic groups, over 900 in Kisumu. The staff was greatly affected by the violence, so the Director contacted David Zarembka asking for one-day workshops so more of their staff could be helped. But AVP and Healing and Rebuilding Our Communities (HROC) both begin with a three-day workshop. So Malesi Kinaro, FPCD Chair Pastor Shamala Joseph, and FPCD Treasurer Janet Ifedha sat down and wrote a one-day curriculum that combined AVP, HROC, and the tree of violence. HROC was included because so many of them were traumatized. Malesi Kinaro tells about those workshops:

"Then we went to Kisumu, but even reaching Kisumu was a problem, because Kisumu was really hot. We were stopped many miles away and then got a taxi to get us around to the hotel because the hotel was safe. We stayed over a month giving the one-day workshops. We alternated facilitating.

"We set the AVP themes up like a mountain: affirmation, communication, collaboration. And then we began the opposite. How do we talk to each other, inter-tribally? They said, 'the Kikuyus are this; the Luos are that.' So from this, how would you communicate? And how would you collaborate?

"Then how about if we changed, because this thing was just the last spark? They agreed that this thing has been there. How about if we affirmed each other? What does affirmation mean? How would we talk to each other? And if we talk to each other like this, how would we grow so we can lose those things like blame. If you are angry, what are some of the things that you can do? That is also an AVP theme, the tree of violence, the tree of nonviolence.

"Then we would ask how they were feeling now and they would say how they were feeling, so we could deal with trauma and its effects, what it does to us. How have you been coping? People would share how they have been coping, how they have not been coping. That would be from HROC. In the afternoon we would look at violence, this cycle of violence.

How can we cut through this circle so it doesn't reach the violence? We would look at early warning signs, all those things. Now we are here. What is the way forward? What am I going to do when I leave this place?

"It was marvelling! We found a complete validation of its power. We could see that it really helped people. People were so confused, so traumatized. The trauma was at its highest, but we helped them to make sense of it." (Malesi Kinaro)

Kisiis/Kipsigis

While FPCD was doing the workshops in Kisumu, they learned that things were really bad in Kisii between the Kipsigis and the Kisiis. These two groups were always fighting, but they really went wild in the post-election violence. The Uzima had been working with youth there, so Malesi mobilized her Uzima Foundation staff, Jared Nyagwoka and George Ongubo, who were already there, as she describes:

"Very many Kisiis had been thrown out of their homes and they were just weird. I was told a mother had to kill a child because the child was coughing and they were being followed. She just covered the child's mouth until it died. So people in Kisii were highly traumatized.

"We decided to be a kind of receiving place because people brought their children to the market and just left them there. Some didn't even know where their family's homes were because this was second generation in the Kisii area. So the children were taken to the IDP camp and our staff was involved with the other people who were working there. The Uzima youth were setting up the camp.

"Then we tried to get them together to talk, but no one would talk to anyone. The Kipsigis said the Kisiis were all bad! And nobody wanted to see anyone from the government because they said government officials are liars. And so we began what we were calling inter-community dialogue.

"If they saw any government official, they would not come, but if they saw just these young people from Uzima, they would come. So the Uzima Foundation youth were the ones that were chairing these meetings. The older folks were just sitting back. But it was chaos—the anger! Everyone was sitting apart. The ones who were not chairing the meetings were sitting with the different groups. Then they bought them some snacks and they ate. When they ate together, that was the first break. But when this was reported in the papers, you never heard about Uzima youth, you only heard about the District Commissioners and the Members of Parliament.

"One day my staff reported that there was no meeting. When they went, they found people with arrows in their bodies. So they hired a vehicle and took them to hospital. Those two Uzima staff were very, very courageous because both of them were Kisiis and they were working in Kipsigis land. So there would have been suspicions, but they worked anyway." (Malesi Kinaro)

Laikipia—Reaching Youth

Getry Agizah was work-ing for FPCD at that time. She was challenged by a young man that generated a new direction of the Friends work. "One day a boy on a bicycle asked me, 'Are you sym-pathizers or are you peace-makers?' I was so pissed off, 'How can you talk like that? Your brothers and sisters have killed people.' I thought  he wanted me not to think about the evidence. But when I went back to my home and was quiet with myself, the ques-tion came back, 'Are you sympathizers or peacemakers?' I realized that I was sympathizing with the IDP individuals. I wasn't looking at the perpetrators who have needs and thoughts to be heard. That's why they did what they did. So I told Malesi that we needed to have a forum for the motorbike and bicycle riders.

"We had that meeting and they talked the whole day. We left that meeting so late. They were expressing their anger about their life. They didn't talk about stealing of votes. They talked about their rights being denied. We left the meeting understanding why Kakamega town burned. People say that Kakamega wasn't that bad, but it was bad." (Getry Agizah)

Coincidentally, Getry Agizah was drawn into a project geared toward Nairobi youth. Kuki Gallmann, an Italian ranch owner on the Laikipia Plateau, had turned her expansive land into a private game ranch. In the midst of the post-election violence, she got a grant to bring city slum-dwelling youth to Laikipia to train them in nonviolence. The only problem was that she had no experience in nonviolence, so she called David Zarembka for help and he called Getry Agizah, who tells about that terrifying experience:

"My response was, 'Do you value my life?' because I felt like he was giving me a death sentence. It was just the day before that they got on a bus in Naivasha and chopped off people's heads. This was a challenge to my life, a challenge to my ministry. But because I looked at David as a father and also a boss, I agreed.

"Kuki Gallmann had mobilized youth from Nairobi slums, from Kibera. I had never interacted with guys with dreadlocks who had killed. I was scared. It was time to use my skills, but I was not confident. We sat around at night talking, even talking about how to kill the President, how to make a bomb, and I was part of that. The following morning I asked them, 'if you wanted to make this Kenya without hurting anybody, how would you do it?'

"They said, 'We don't know what we can do.' Then I don't know what happened, if it was God, but something happened and there was a shift. They were now looking at a new society and that was an AVP society-building exercise. They created a series of societies, a mountain society, a farming society, a sea society. The sea one would have fish; farming society would plant crops; and the mountain society would have animals. The question was, how would each society survive? So they developed a society and they had to make a declaration by the end of the workshop so they said, 'We will never be used again.'" (Getry Agizah, FCPT Coordinator)

Bicycle Race

Another effort to reach the youth was a bicycle race on May 17, 2008, from Chekalini to Turbo. Pastor Simon Bulimo explains: "We organized the youth coming together. FCPT assisted with a bicycle race. They brought their own bicycles, but we provided a T-shirt. There were youth from different tribes, Luhya, Kalenjin, Luo, Kikuyu, in the same race." (Simon Bulimo, Friends Pastor)

FCPT

From February through April of 2008 the FCPT concentrated on humanitarian assistance and listening to the needs of the internally displaced people (IDPs). FCPT decided to focus on the smaller camps that were skipped by the Red Cross and other larger organizations. In each visit they brought what humanitarian supplies they could, but it was never enough. The need was overwhelming because the people had fled with only the clothes on their backs. Here are a few examples from their back-to-office reports.

Lumakanda

In Lumakanda the IDPs were in the police station first. But there were not enough latrines, so they were moved to the primary school where their numbers grew to over 2,500. When school started later in January, they were moved to the IDP camp in Turbo.

Margaret Wanyonyi describes the first time she went to visit the IDPs in Lumakanda. "Personally, I went there, but on the way I was telling Gladys Kamonya, 'I don't feel like going to see those people because I will start shedding tears.' Gladys said, 'We are going there, but don't ever shed tears.'

"But when I reached there, I kept asking myself, 'Why should these people suffer here? Why should they leave their homes and suffer here? It was chaotic!'

"When they saw me, those who knew me said, 'So, you can think about us. You have even come to see where we are.' They were so happy, but I could not talk to them because I was crying.

"I pulled myself together to encourage them. I told them, 'You take heart. This will end. You are not going to live here forever. If you get time, you can come to visit us.'

"They could not go to their homes; they had been burned to ashes. So, they came to visit us and we gave them food and clothes." (Margaret Wanyonyi)

Machewa, Kiminini, and Sabatia

The first three team visits organized by the FCPT were on the 7th of February. The team leaders reported at the next FCPT meeting, the 9th of February. Visits to camps began with a prayer and a talk by one of the FCPT members who explained about Friends' work to help the IDPs. Representatives of the IDPs spoke and then relief was distributed.

At the Machewa Chief's camp there were five units with committees set up to oversee humanitarian response. The team split up and interviewed groups of people: disabled, women, youth, and elderly. The IDPs indicated that they needed assistance with school fees, finance, food, farm inputs, blankets, textbooks, and counselling. One woman said that her husband was killed during the violence; another did not know the whereabouts of her husband.

One youth said that he witnessed several of his friends being killed. He requested seeds and fertilizer during the planting season. Another youth could not trace his parents, brothers and sisters. He too requested farm inputs.

One man asked FCPT to come up with a trauma healing programme. He warned that their desperate conditions

Wesley Sasita with the Machewa Chief

Relief supplies procured by FCPT for humanitarian relief

Raymond Ojiambo

IDPs line up to get humanitarian supplies from FCPT workers

Raymond Ojiambo

FCPT members Simon Bulimo, Dorothy Selebwa, and Joseph Mamai
deliver blankets to IDPs who had been sleeping on the open ground.

can easily force them into doing things that compromise our African culture, referring to prostitution and the spread of HIV/AIDS.

Eric Lijodi wrote in his back-to-office-report, "The committee that is led by this area chief has a clear record. ... The area has a well set-up structure that responds to the various needs of the IDPs."

The second group on the 7th of February went first to the District Officer of Saboti, but that situation was not conducive to IDPs, because there was mistrust. They left two bags of maize and twelve blankets, and went to the Kiminini Market to Deliverance Church where there were 661 families and Toba Vunja Church where there were 80 families. They asked for humanitarian assistance and counselling.

The third group on the 7th of February went to Sabatia that had 259 families with 1,858 people. They distributed blankets to the elderly and children, but left other items with the chief, even though it seemed that the IDPs trusted the peace team more than the local administrators. They asked for food, blankets, soap, sugar, salt, medication, and counselling.

After assessing their funds, the FCPT assigned particular members to purchase maize, beans, rice, cooking fat, salt, sugar, blankets, and soap. They had originally decided to buy 40 bags of maize, but the lorry could hold 99, so that was what was purchased.

Milembe, Chwele, Kimilili

On 19th February 2008, a team of 11 FCPT members visited the Milembe Camp. IDPs came from three settlement farms and were being hosted by three Friends: John Kitui, Joseph Lumbasi, and Cliffe. At one time the Friends Church at Milembe was attacked and its windows broken. Mzee John Kitui of that church said that he didn't know the whereabouts of some of his pastors as they had run for safety. He reported that the Endebe camp had much congestion with 6,800 IDPs and that what we are experiencing is not a political crisis, but a land crisis that has been boiling on for quite some time. He said the government response to the IDPs is very poor.

Raymond Ojiambo

FCPT members confer with the Chief at Chwele over lists of IDPs

Raymond Ojiambo

IDPs in the camp at Chwele

"Distribution of the relief items was quite hectic for us. Many of the IDPs were literally scrambling for what we were providing. The balance of the relief items we had were handed over to Mzee John Kitui to distribute on a later day." (back-to-office report by Eric Lijodi)

When a FCPT team of 11 members went to Chwele IDP Centre on the 18th March 2008, ten additional members of Chwele Yearly Meeting joined them. General Secretary of the Yearly Meeting Stephen Kisiangani indicated there were 430 IDPs from five different camps attending the meeting. Three representatives of the IDPs spoke, explaining how they were chased away from their homes in Mt. Elgon, victims of the Sabaot Land Defence Force. They have no place to sleep, no food, and some of their children were not going to school. Young girls were resorting to working in hostile conditions that expose them to sexually-transmitted diseases. They requested medical care.

The distribution of food and other items was fraught with difficulties. The FCPT team was given lists of names that were manipulated with some names appearing on more than one list and favouritism involved. Some of the names were church members instead of IDPs and some church members were hiding items in the church. People were very unruly and forced their way through the gate making the distribution of relief come to a standstill.

On 18th March 2008 another FCPT team visited the Kimilili Centre, which was at Kimilili Friends Church. The crowd was estimated at 1500. The IDPs were from Mt. Elgon (Kapsoro) Gitwamba. They were staying with friends or relatives or were renting houses. One woman from Napororoa Pentecostal Church said she had welcomed nine people in her home, which greatly strained her family's resources and would appreciate any help the FCPT could give.

A man from Kapsoro said that the people of Kimilili were treating them with kindness. He suggested that an independent group be established where the IDPs could give their sentiments in confidence. And, he suggested that a committee of representatives should be formed to oversee the distribution of humanitarian assistance because the current committees were not giving out everything meant for the IDPs.

There was a rush for food and so much pushing that two women fainted. The team requested assistance from three policemen and the food was carried into the church and only a few were allowed in at a time. The team stayed until everyone had been served and discovered that the committee had reserved for themselves approximately one-quarter of the food items brought by the team.

In his back-to-office report, Joseph Mamai Makokha wrote, "Our effort to assist the displaced is being fought against by these people. It is my strong recommendation that we make a deliberate effort to distribute these items ourselves to the last drop before leaving the centres. What the IDPs complain about, that they are denied their shares, was confirmed."

Eldoret/Turbo

Wilson Ngairia was Clerk of the Eldoret Monthly Meeting during the time of the 2007 election.

"On Sunday the first of January, 2008, I saw people coming with children and luggage to our church. They were saying, "there is violence in our place. We can't stay there."

We were shocked and then we looked for a peaceful way to help these people. We called the members around and they said, "we can come with some food; we can come with porridge for the children." Little by little we began to help. Through our brother called Bainito, we got support. They sent us some money to buy some food for the people who were in our church.

"These people who were being chased away were Kikuyu. We really prayed to God and asked God to protect us because our Friends church stands for the peace testimony. If they decide to burn the church, let it happen. We could not chase these people away, we must protect these people. Those we felt were in danger, especially the Kikuyu tribe, we used some money to give them transportation to their safe place, to the Central Province as they had requested, because they didn't have money. Those who were Luhyas, Kalenjins, or Luos, we kept in the church and we were providing them food and all that. We got police protection for them. The police came to the church. The Friends Church Peace Team was giving them some support, food stuffs, detergent, all of that. Even some of them became members of our church, saying, "you people have treated us well and we are not even members, so we will become members of this church." Even those who are not Luhyas have become members, so the church is now more diverse.

"I am an AVP facilitator. I have organized workshops. CAPI has been supporting us. We organized community forums to bring Kalenjins and Kikuyus together so they can interact and understand each other. I have brought some of the youth to be trained in AVP. Some have trained to the facilitator level, so they are now facilitators. I have taken some to the mediation training and some are involved in Turning the Tide so they can be activist drivers. And at the personal level, some are friends. They are transformed people.

"I think the next election will be peaceful, especially in the Turbo Division. We are targeting the young people, especially in Eldoret. I think CAPI has really helped us. They have supported us to do workshops in those border areas. We are expecting that they will not take sides during the elections of 2013.

"We are expecting that CAPI will support us to conduct more workshops on civic education so that we can train people what it is all about. It is better that we do not wait, but facilitate civic education. We did some civic education supported by the National Council of Churches of Kenya before the charges were to be announced by the International Criminal Court (ICC). They gave us funds to mobilize people to understand what the ICC is all about. The Member of Parliament from our area, William Ruto, was one of the six who might be charged. The feeling in the community was that taking Ruto to the ICC was like taking all Kalenjins to the ICC. But we explained that, "no, no, no, this is an issue of an individual, not a community nor a country. When the results were announced on January 23rd and Ruto was charged, they didn't take it as a community, but as an individual. So there was no violence associated with the announcement of the charges."

FCPT helped 15,000 IDPs

From February through April of 2008, FCPT assisted approximately 15,000 IDPs. FCPT Chairman Joseph Mamai Makokha summed up the humanitarian assistance:

"From February through April we concentrated on humanitarian assistance. Where we went, we never went back, because it was not enough. We couldn't go back because it was overwhelming to us. We wanted to cover as big an area as possible, from Eldoret to Kisumu, where there are Friends churches. But we didn't just give to Friends. Whoever we found in the camp we took care of that person. We went to

the smaller camps of less than 400 people that had not been visited. These big organisations never cared about them. Our committee comprised people from various areas. When we met, we would say, 'where can we go next?' Someone would say, 'Let's go here, let's go there.' It helped us to identify these small camps. It was not enough. I don't think it would have carried them for even one week, but we thought it was better than nothing." (Joseph Mamai Makokha, FCPT Chair)

"During the time we were dealing with humanitarian assistance, it was amazing to see how tight the loop was of action, reflection, and learning. We were people who had no professional background in humanitarian aid. We were entirely self-educated. We would meet weekly, figure out where we were going and what we needed to carry with us, and reflect on what we did the previous week. There was so much learning that was packed into that period as we tried to figure out stuff that professional humanitarian organizations already know. How do you prevent the lady in the red skirt from coming through the line three times? It was exhilarating." (Eden Grace, FUM Field Officer)

Kaimosi

Moses Masika tells of the work of the students at Friends Theological College:

"John Muhanji came and addressed us. Everything was full of peace, create peace, preach peace, and work peace. Wherever you meet, talk about peace and encourage people not to fight. Muhanji and the group arranged for us to visit some of the IDP camps. We met a Sub-Chief at Chevarenga about a kilometre from Kaimosi. That camp had about 2,000 people from Nandi in the Rift Valley, people who had been displaced. Some of them had lost relatives.

"The first day we went in the morning. We were about 30 students from the college. We carried some sugar, maize, oil, and T-shirts that had been donated from Friends in the U.S. But before we distributed the materials, Muhanji preached for about 45 minutes. After preaching, he said, 'can you mix with these people to encourage them?' Their testimonies were painful. They explained and then we knew, this person has been affected. We came back with some food and clothing and continued coordinating with the Chief. We found out that those people we had been guiding and counselling had identified people who had killed their relatives or stolen their cattle. About three families had a reconciliation service at the same centre with the people who had stolen from them. Those were the only families we saw going back to their land. They shared all their grief and forgave each other and then they went back." (Moses Masika)

In the post-election violence, Kaimosi Hospital was extremely busy. They had many patients from the nearby Nandi District, where people were using poisoned spears and arrows.

Matron Irene Gulavi explains: "We had many patients that had arrows all over their bodies: intestine, foot, brain. We even had one man with an arrow in his brain. We had to remove them in our theatre.

"Many people's houses were burned and people were displaced. We kept some people here to feed them. There was a family we had to keep for awhile feeding them until we found a home for them.

"We had a lot of instability in the schools. There was a Nandi school boy who killed another school boy from this side, a Luhya. They had bought land on the Nandi side. We heard so many frightening stories. The hospital was working hard both day and night, stitching wounds and taking people to the theatre to remove arrows. The community was quite frightened, but eventually we overcame it." (Irene Gulavi, Head Matron, Kaimosi Hospital)

Mobile Clinic

Matron Irene Gulavi joined the first trip from Kaimosi to Turbo when the FCPT counselling group included students from Friends Theological College. She describes her experience: "The first time it was just counselling. We put them in groups, men, women, youth, etc. We found a very depressed community. As they talked, they cried, both men and women were weeping. They had lost husbands, or wives and children. Houses were being burned with the people still inside, but they had done nothing. In Turbo there was a woman who told me that all her maize stores were burned; all her animals were taken away; and her house was burned. It was a permanent home and someone came and burned her house to ashes. She had lived in that place for more than 60 years. She went there when she was very young and now she is old. Where can such a person go?

"It was very bad, so the second time we looked for money from the Christian Health Association of Kenya (CHAK). They gave us money and we bought drugs. I mobilized a big outreach group of nurses, clinical staff, voluntary counselling and testing group, eight people altogether.

"First we did a tour. We split up and went all around the camp. There were 7,000 people in that camp and some of them were very sick. We found that the latrines were full of stool and urine. The tents were wet because there was a lot of rain. Some areas were very wet and people were very sick. Tuberculosis patients were not able to get their drugs.

"The food was being rationed. It was given by the National Youth Service and it was little. We discovered those who were very ill were not getting the right food stuffs, like diabetics, tuberculosis patients, undernourished children. The diet was just flat. You might get only rice with oil, but you would not get egg or anything else.

"We found naked children who didn't have clothing. We found poor classrooms. Somebody had put up a structure for a school within that camp. The classes were poor. Children were sitting on a wood floor; the teacher had no chalkboard, but they were learning. The children looked very anxious. It was not a good sight. I still see it. Everyone lacked medical care; there was no medical care for all those people.

"So we settled to give medical care. After we had identified the problems, we started out by treating minor illnesses such as pneumonia, malaria, and coughs. Those were the ones that we could treat. We were able to refer those who were seriously ill to the hospital at Eldoret or Webuye. We did testing. Some of the people were HIV-positive and some of them were alright. We did not reach back to Kaimosi until 10 pm." (Irene Gulavi, Head Matron, Kaimosi Hospital)

Agatha Ganira was a counsellor on that team: "To talk about it brings back bad memories. I was not prepared for what was there. It was so bad. We did what we could and prayed with them, and tried to encourage them.

"I did the HIV testing and counselling. Some of the women wanted to know their status because they had been victims of sexual abuse during the violence, but we didn't know if they had gotten the virus there or before.

Some were already positive and had been on the anti-retroviral drugs (ARV) treatment, but lacked the drugs. They didn't know which regime they were on and their documents burned up with their houses. We did not have the ARV, so we told people they had to go to the hospital to get them. But the people were afraid to go to the hospital. There was a shortage of condoms in the camp and some women said they had to have sex just to survive.

"It was overwhelming. I couldn't go again because of burn-out. We had a debriefing with CHAK, which helped me." (Agatha Ganira, Coordinator of Comprehensive Care Unit of the Kaimosi Hospital)

Friends Humanitarian Assistance in Nairobi

Friends in Nairobi concentrated their humanitarian work in Kibera, a slum in Nairobi, and in Nakuru, a smaller city in the Rift Valley where large numbers of IDPs were housed in a large stadium. Churchill Kibisu describes the early humanitarian work in Nairobi:

"Besides the Pastoral Letter, our other approach was to help those affected by the violence, especially in Kibera, which was really bad. We sought assistance for food for those who were displaced. The response was quite overwhelming because many people brought food for those in the camps. We received support from Britain Yearly Meeting, FUM, Friends Church in Kenya, and from Friends in the U.S.

"We concentrated on Nakuru and Kibera. We bought food. We used the Friends International Centre and the churches as distribution points. People came here for rations. It was fairly orderly. But after awhile women carrying food home to Kibera were attacked by young men who stole the food. After that we got coupons from the supermarkets, which we gave out so the people could buy their own food. In Kibera the Catholics also joined the effort. We used the small churches in Kibera. We also provided counselling.

"We had to identify who was in need, especially in Nakuru. For that we relied on members on the ground, or community leaders. In Nakuru the people were in the stadium from January through part of February. Then we relied on political solutions because the effort could not be sustained. We exhausted our resources.

"We continued providing food almost the whole year, but the crucial time was January through March. It became very expensive for us, but whenever we got some funding, we provided food." (Churchill Kibisu, Assistant Presiding Clerk, FUM)

Uzima Foundation youth in Nairobi were working in the Kibera slum at the height of the violence. Rupert Watson, co-executor of the George Drew estate, not only supported the work financially, but was himself a part of the mediation team with the Uzima youth.

Cornelius Ambiah was one of those directly involved in Friends humanitarian work organized by CAPI. "Immediately after the post-election violence we did a tour of the IDP camps. When we went to Kikuyu, a place not far from here, I was given a group of 18. What helped me is that I know about trauma. When you are lead-  ing people, you are not supposed to cry with people. You are supposed to strengthen them. If I broke down in tears, there would be no one to lead. It was just a sharing of what happened to you. It was so moving because when each young person started speaking, they had to cry. We had to take some pauses just to give them time to relax so that they could compose themselves and keep on sharing what they wanted to share.

"When we went there we had some food stuffs, but what stood out for me was that we were not just there to give them food, but to give them emotional support. Trying to tell them, 'you are living here today, but you never know. You may be the President of this country, so don't lose hope.' To make them feel like they are still wanted, they are still human beings, that the kind of environment that they were living in is not an obstacle for them to still be strong and able to see whatever are their desires in life." (Cornelius Ambiah)

In 2012 there are still IDPs living in camps. The goal of the government is to resettle them all before the next election.

"The transition from humanitarian assistance to reconciliation was a very powerful moment when we had a very clear idea of what we were doing and why." (Eden Grace)

The next chapter describes the reconciliation work of Friends.

CHAPTER SIX
Political Resolution and Friends Reconciliation Work
Political Resolution of the Crisis

While Friends were providing humanitarian assistance to IDPs, international diplomats were trying to help the Kenyan leaders to come to a political resolution of the crisis of the 2007 Kenya election. Initially Desmond Tutu of South Africa, U.S. Assistant Secretary of State for African Affairs Jendayi Frazer, and President of the African Union John Kufuor came but were not successful in achieving a solution to the crisis. However, John Kufuor persuaded Kofi Annan to lead an African delegation, which included Graca Machel of South Africa and the former President of Tanzania, Benjamin Mkapa.

Beginning January 23rd, the African delegation met with both sides separately and then together until an agreement was reached. As there were allegations of election rigging on both sides and no means at hand to resolve the question of who actually won the election, power sharing seemed the best solution. Ironically, the structure of that solution was what had been agreed between Kibaki and Odinga before the 2002 election, where Kibaki would be the President and Odinga the Prime Minister. The cabinet was expanded to include ODM members. The agreement was signed on February 28, 2008.

Trauma Healing and CounsellingWestern Kenya

Alternatives to Violence Project (AVP—*see Appendix for details of programmes and Friends organizations*) training had started formally in Kenya in 2003 under the Change Agents for Peace Programme (CAPP). A few AVP workshops had been held among Friends both in Nairobi and in western Kenya over the next two years (2003–2005) as resources allowed. Realizing that trauma healing and counselling were needed, FCPT contacted the 64 Friends in Kenya who had already been trained in AVP. Of these, 13 Friends volunteered, along with three members of FCPT, to attend a two-day workshop at the Lubao Peace Centre where they developed a work plan for counselling and trauma healing in western Kenya. They decided to concentrate on two areas that were greatly affected, Turbo and Mt. Elgon. The team of counsellors included 40 people trained in AVP.

Turbo

Visits to the camps began with a prayer and an encouraging talk by Joseph Mamai Makokha, Chair of FCPT, explaining about Friends being a peace church. Then the IDPs were divided into groups, women, youth, children, disabled, elderly, etc., and the FCPT members listened to the individuals in the smaller groups. Here are a few examples of the back to office reports from the 21st April 2008 visit to Turbo Camp:

Children under seven years told Humphreys Ambasa of their needs, most of which related to school. "Rulers, uniforms, exercise books, shoes, socks, rubbers for erasing, pens, pencils, textbooks, bags for carrying their books, pullovers (sweaters) for coldness, umbrella, chalk and duster in the classroom, soap, clothes. Food is given but is not enough.

"At the beginning there were more than 30 teachers, but later almost half ran away. Why? No salary. Those who are still working (15) need textbooks for the pupils, teachers' reference textbooks. They are understaffed. They have up to 100 pupils in a class for one teacher. Most of them are not paid." (Humphreys Ambasa)

Eunice Okwemba listened to children under 12 years old tell of their experiences. "One boy of 10 years said they used to stay at Musembe village when they were attacked by unknown people who chased them away from home. They went and spent the first night in the forest where they were also chased away and landed at Lumakanda Police Station.

"One girl said her family were chased from Kipkarren River only to be picked up by police who later brought them to the IDP camp.

"Another girl said that they were robbed of everything and her grandmother was beaten to death.

"'Kikuyus are thieves, they stole the votes,' were the words of one boy in Class VI who is at the IDP camp with his family after vacating from Murgu near Mwamba.

"Another boy shared his story of being chased away, property stolen and is now at the IDP with his parents.

"Another boy told us that he was sent to the shop and he met young men on the way. They followed him to his house and ordered them to leave the house. Their house was burnt down and property lost in the violence. They were rescued by Lumakanda police who later brought them to the IDP in Turbo.

"A girl from Mwamba had to run to Kitale for shelter after their house was burnt. Her father was almost thrown in a borehole [well], but he cried for help.

"A boy from Sango lost his father in the violence.

"The requests of all these children were that they don't have proper sanitation, proper education, enough teachers, books and, also, they are not sure of their future. They had one thing in common as a request. They need standard education.

"One boy asked, 'Why is it that the Kikuyus are the only ones who were being chased away? Why are we being called thieves and some of us didn't vote or steal? For how long shall we continue staying in the camp? Shall we be relocated some place not here?'

"They were very touching stories and I couldn't hold my tears. These innocent children are really suffering. These are but a few of the sharings that I was able to take because there were very many children and I couldn't interview all of them. I hope something good will happen to change these lives." (Eunice Okwemba)

Simon Indago "was chosen to listen to the youth about the problems they face in the camp. The youth are traumatized badly. They lack jobs to make up their future. During food giving, they are thrown out of line. They are stressed because of idleness in the camp. They have lost their jobs, business, land, houses, and goods.

"Some have started drinking alcohol, taking opium, and drug abuse. Some say that they are sick mentally. They asked me if they can be assisted by books, old newspapers, TVs, radios and other entertainment to keep them busy in the camp. They said they have visited their neighbours, but they chased them away from their *shamba* [field]. So, it is not possible to go back to their land. They urge Friends in Peace and the government to look for the solution of peace with the neighbours.

"They told me these reports should not be kept quiet, but we should forward them to responsible officials to work for immediate effect. They add that others have lost their parents in the camp. They are crying to leaders to help them solve these matters." (Simon Indago)

Pamela Masitsa listened to a group of women. They said that "People were ejected out of their land by their neighbours that they knew very well. Their residential homes and homesteads were destroyed and burned. Property was destroyed, including food, livestock, houses, households worth thousands of shillings. Trees, bananas, fruits like avocado, oranges, etc., were destroyed. Looting of property by the youth was arranged by local leaders. It seemed there was some sponsorship from the well known people (politicians).

"The women's basic needs were shelter, bedding, clothing, petticoats, underwear, sanitary pads, braziers, drugs for those on medication, school fees, love from spouses, and food.

"They said they will not be allowed by the locals to go back and have their businesses. Most of them promised not to go back to their farms because of very high hatred. They want the President, the Prime Minister, and other political leaders to come to the camp so they can address the problems. Some want to be compensated so they can go to other areas where they can live in peace. Few members wished for reconciliation." (Pamela Masitsa)

Merciline Mirembe shared with six children and two women. "The government must give them maximum protection and justice. The feelings were that if they were taken back to their land they are not safe in view of the present circumstances. They feel that the government should look for alternatives rather than former places that are insecure.

"Most of the children complained of the bad weather, clothing, feeding and utensils. Others needed rubber shoes to protect them from chiggers. Classes were filled with water during the rainy season which made the situation very difficult for the victims.

"Teachers were working voluntarily without pay for the last three months. Most of them had only one dress; they lost most of their property. Generally the environment was not conducive for proper learning." (Merciline Mirembe)

Jody Richmond and Rose Imbega interviewed ten men. "One man had lived at his place since the year 1965. He left on 29th December 2007 immediately after the announcement of election. No house remained. All were demolished down; even cows were taken away. He lost all his properties.

"He visited his farm recently. They took the iron sheets, windows and doors. The people who did that were busy now using the iron sheets to build their own houses.

"This morning he went back to check if he would be able to work on his farm. He talked to his neighbour if he can clean his compound and the farm. The neighbour agreed to assist him and he left the neighbour some money for the work to be done. The neighbour also informed him that things were not so bad. A "Good Samaritan" had started farming for him, while another neighbour had taken part of his land and began farming without authority. He talked to that neighbour peacefully and he surrendered the part he had taken. He even gave him seeds and fertilizer. He is ready to go back to his farm if the government can provide good security for him.

"The problem with youth, if they look at you, their eyes show as if they want to fight again. We appeal to the government if they can protect us with enough security, otherwise going back to our farms or houses will be very difficult because our lives will be in danger. We also want the government to assist us with seeds and fertilizer, building materials, etc. We shall have no food next year.

"Another man was a Luhya, 32 years old, working with Kikuyus selling blankets and clothes. He felt his life was in danger to go back and work with Kikuyus again. It is not good to stay in the IDP camp. If the government can allocate them a safe place like Sango, where there is a peaceful environment, he can go and stay there. Or, they can give them money to purchase land, a quarter or half an acre. He has already forgiven those people who destroyed people's properties.

"Most of the IDPs in our group suggested that there is a need for the peace team to approach the government and tell them the problems people living in the IDP camps are having. They are suffering a lot.

"They also requested that the peace team visit them again and talk to them. The time did not allow us to listen to all of their sad stories. At the end of the session we prayed together with them. One of them who was a pastor prayed.

"They all said they have forgiven those people who destroyed everything of theirs. God bless them all." (Jody Richmond and Rose Imega)

Among the counsellors were students in Jody Richmond's class at the Friends Theological College. Frances Kutima was one of those students: "At the time I was taking a class on Peace and Conflict. I had already been trained in AVP and I had some psychology classes, so we went out to Turbo to do trauma counselling. The people were not so friendly at first. But the local officials recommended us and they knew we were there to help. First we met with them in general and then divided them into groups and talked with them individually. Some individuals told us they could not disclose what had happened." (Frances Kutima)

Listening to the Perpetrators

FCPT realized that they had only been counselling the IDPs, but the other side, the perpetrators, really needed some healing, too. They had six listening sessions with the Nandi communities in the Turbo area and one with Luhya in Lugari District. These sessions were very tense because the people were very hostile at first, but the counselling group persisted and eventually made some progress.

David Zarembka explains that the FCPT Counselling Committee had their own sessions: "Jody Richmond of Friends Theological College led training sessions before and after our sessions with the Nandis. We were wondering whether we should give our names, because they would know we were all Luhyas. But then we decided that we couldn't hide who we are.

"Another issue was how to avoid reacting to what was being said in the listening sessions. We did a role play to work on this. At first we were listening to a Luhya describe their experiences and everyone was relaxed and smiling. Then it was a Nandi talking and suddenly the listeners became tense and had worried looks on their faces. We realized that we must not do that in the listening sessions, that body language is very important." (David Zarembka, AGLI Coordinator)

In her back-to-office report, Phyllis Wanjala said that at first the Nandis were hostile and listed all the reasons that Kikuyus were not wanted by the other tribes:

IDPs assemble for a listening session with FCPT members at Cheptulu

FCPT member Dorothy Selenbwa speaks to IDPs in Cheptulu

"They don't have respect towards some other tribes. They are very proud, rude, because of the President being Kikuyu, saying that the work of the Nandis are to look after cattle and sell milk, and the Luhyas marrying, eating ugali, being watchmen, and cooks. During the last election, the Kikuyus never voted for Councillor and MP, but only for President, who is their fellow Kikuyu. The Kikuyus never associate with some other tribes, even when they want to buy something like sugar or soda, they will never make the mistake of buying from a non-Kikuyu. Life to them is not worthy, only property.

"The youth were the most affected and are many. The youth are idle, that is why they were burning and looting. They wanted a change, ODM, not PNU, so when we talk about peace, it is important to involve the youths because they are the majority in the community, and the most wounded ones.

"The way forward if the government wants people to reconcile and resettle those who are in the camps:

1) Let the government resettle people one tribe after another.

2) Release those [Nandi youth] who are in jail.

3) Income of the country must be shared equally.

4) Create employment for the youth who are idle."

Resettlement

By May of 2008 the Kenya government announced that it was time to send all the IDPs home and close the camps. This announcement threw the local administrators into a panic because they had no idea how to accomplish this. Because FCPT had been listening to both the IDPs and the communities that had chased them away from their homes, Friends were called to help with the resettlement.

In order to resettle the IDPs back in their home communities, Friends realized they needed a new vocabulary. The IDPs had been thought of as the victims and those who chased them away were referred to as "perpetrators." So, they created new terms, "returning community" and "receiving community."

John Muhanji was called by the Turbo District Commissioner (DC) at midnight on Sunday, May 15, 2008, asking for his help to move the IDPs at the Eldoret show grounds back to their homes. The DC explained that the IDPs were hostile to him and the only people who could help them were the Friends Church, so John called together a group from FCPT. John Muhanji describes what happened:

"We went to the IDP camp and met with the people. When I talked and prayed for them, they went willingly and

 started pulling down their tents ready to leave to their new station, which was closer to their houses that had been destroyed. Lorries (trucks) were provided to carry them to the place. Meanwhile we went to see the place where they were relocating. We found that there were no rest rooms or water nearby. At this time the DC had left us with the District Officer

(DO). We called the DC and asked him to provide funds for the toilets and water, but he never came to us again.

"Time was moving and nothing was taking place, so I called Eden Grace in FUM's Kisumu office and asked her to send me 40,000 Kenya shillings ($667) to use for the process. Eden responded very fast, and I started rolling things into action. The toilets were put in place. I bought pipes to connect the water, which was 200 meters from the location. I also provided food to those people who did this work. I enabled the connection of electricity from a nearby hospital to provide light for security. I got 200 metres of wire and its accessories. It was as if I had calculated the exact amount that was required for the work.

"I left the camp at 8:45 pm when the camp had water, rest rooms, and lights in a very short time. The IDPs and the DO felt encouraged and supported. The people felt that indeed the Friends Church is a true peace church that cared for them. They commented that we had been very helpful in the process. They saw integrity in us and wished this church could stay with them all the time. I felt encouraged and energised to see that we could offer a new life of hope to people who have been feeling hopeless."

Some resettlements went even better than that one. Joshua Lilande led an FCPT group to resettle IDPs in the Jua Kali receiving community on the 19th of May. They expected to prepare a camp for the IDPs as their homes had been burned and the receiving community had been very hostile when the Friends first visited them, saying they never wanted the Kikuyus to come back. But as they listened to the FCPT, they softened, so that by the time the IDPs arrived, there was a reconciliation spirit and the receiving community took the IDPs into their own homes.

Joseph Mamai was with the FCPT team resettling IDPs from the Turbo camp to the Sugoi area and describes that experience: "We wanted to know how ready the IDPs were to go back to their home. They said they were very ready, but whoever had driven them away from their homes were still there. They wanted security that they would be accepted. They asked us to go talk to the people who had driven them away to see if they would accept them. 'If they say they would accept us, we would go this evening, because we are tired of staying in these camps where life is hectic. Imagine someone who had all his wealth in the millions, now finding himself in a tent, it is difficult!'

"So the FCPT team went to the receiving community. At first they talked violently; they did not want to hear about the returning community. They told us, 'if you bring these people, we will stone you.' But we were lucky, we were patient. They poured out their anger, giving the shortcomings of these other people, how they behave, why they should not come back again.

"God gave us the language to use, 'Not all of them are bad. Today it is them. Tomorrow it may be you. How would you feel staying away from your own home in a tent?' Later on they said they would only accept those who are good. They wouldn't accept all of them. 'We will go to the camp and show you who we will bring. Please don't force us to bring the others.'

"We promised them we would not force them. We all climbed into the lorries and went to the Turbo camp. They picked this one, that one. Whoever was picked went into the lorry and was brought to Sugoi. What surprised me most was that some of the receiving community members who had driven these people away, accepted the returning people into their own homes. The following morning they assisted them to rebuild their houses. At first they chose only a few, in a group of 60, 20 were chosen. But I understand later on many more went back. I thought that was a very big achievement."

Trauma Healing and Counselling—Nairobi

Friends in Nairobi also realized that trauma healing was a critical need. Pastor David Irungu is a pastor to the people of the slum area of Kibera: "We followed up with the families, reconciliation, peace work between the communities. One community was being victimized, the Kikuyu, so we started some programmes for them to understand each other. We had some meetings in Kibera so they would not fight again. Peace and reconciliation takes a long time. The issues were more than the politics, but became tribal and differences between those who have and those who have not. Those "have-nots" took advantage and came from Kibera to go and loot. The situation brought out the fact that there are some very poor people.

"Since we were helping them with food it was easy for us to get them to listen to us. Both sides were listening to us, so we were able to bring them together. The National Council of Churches of Kenya helped and the Peace Committee of the Catholic Church.

"We had a lot of successes. We were able to hold meetings of the warring groups and created counselling groups. We trained facilitators from those communities through CAPI. In fact, we continue to train. The communities came together and said, "we cannot forget, but we can forgive." In the slums there were women who were raped. They knew who were their attackers. They said they could forgive, but they could not forget what had happened to them.

"The counselling programme has been very effective. Some of the youths testify that they know they were being used. We have counselling and training sessions with them in the evenings, Bible study, Wednesday fellowship, and Sunday they go to church. The counsellors include two pastors, five evangelists, some lay leaders and student pastors. The women have their own programme. Even before this we had an HIV-AIDS programme in Kibera, so they had confidence in the Friends Church." (Pastor David Irungu)

The AVP and HROC workshops in Nairobi and Nakuru were at first coordinated by CAPI. Then in 2010 the AVP-Trust was able to hire a part-time Coordinator, Wambui Nguyo. They are working in several large slum areas, including Kibera and Mathare.

"Our aim after going through the basic, the advanced, and the training of trainers level is to pick a group of facilitators who can help us to spread the message of AVP and HROC farther. We have about 20 who are facilitators and a few of them are lead facilitators. They start out as apprentices; then they become facilitators; and then they become full lead facilitators. The lead facilitators work with those who have

Nairobi AVP and HROC Failitators, February 4 2012

just been trained and mentor them so they can become full facilitators. We trained another 11 who are now apprentices. They also have to have gone through the therapy. They get a small stipend when they facilitate a workshop." (Wambui Nguyo)

Friends realized that the HROC trauma healing often opens wounds and makes the participants very vulnerable. They didn't feel it was right to just leave them that way, so follow-up individual counselling is offered free of charge in Nairobi. Individuals who are identified as very traumatized in the AVP and HROC workshops are recommended for further individual counselling to a group of professionals organized by Heidi Pidcoke. Many are trained in the trauma therapy called "Eye Movement Desensitization and Reprocessing." They volunteer their time, so the programme is very cost-effective. It is supported by donations from San Francisco Friends Monthly Meeting. Wambui Nguyo describes this programme:

"We give them a questionnaire about trauma before and after the workshop with a scale of one to four on symptoms of trauma. Are you jumpy, etc. We compare the two to see if the trauma levels have gone up after the workshop or have gone down. But anybody who is showing trauma, we recommend them to see a counsellor. Then we brief the counsellor on what the person has been experiencing and leave them to do their work. It is very confidential. They meet with Heidi or someone under her supervision. The one who is doing the therapy can judge if this person needs more than the five sessions that we recommend.

"The follow-up counselling has been successful with those people who finish their counselling, but it has been challenging to get them to finish. Here we have that mentality that for you to see a counsellor, you are not OK. We have to tell them that it doesn't mean that you are not OK. Just come and do the counselling for however long it takes because it is free. HROC will take care of the bills because Heidi has this pool of counsellors who have signed up to give back to the community. Those who have gone through and been helped, they are very, very grateful to HROC. Some of them even want to take HROC farther, to become one of the facilitators." (Wambui Nguyo, AVP Coordinator).

CAPI works with a network of Kibera women working on how to address the violence. Hezron Masitsa explains that "they are mostly HIV-positive. The chairperson is well informed and her leadership skills are bearing fruits. We have trained the group in AVP and HROC. They are learning tailoring and sewing tablemats, which they sell and the proceeds are ploughed back to sustain the group.

"They have had listening events. They share with each other, supporting the HIV-positive women and peace-building. They said they had no place to sit for the listening and, good luck, Jean Smith who works with women in Western, gave them money to buy a tent. So when the tent is up three times per week, there is someone there to listen. With those women, you give them an idea and they take it forward. Counselling is so professionalized and expensive, but here someone is available to listen without the women having to pay." (Hezron Masitsa, CAPI Programs Director)

Mt. Elgon Resettlement

In Mt. Elgon the resettlement has taken much longer, because the violence there had started earlier and continued over several years before 2007. In 2012 some people are just returning to their homes, having been gone for four years.

FCPT decided that the people there needed to focus on healing from the trauma, so rather than AVP, HROC workshops were offered.

Eunice Okwemba was a facilitator in three workshops in two communities in Mt. Elgon that finished a HROC series: "In HROC we have three stages: remembrance, mourning, and the recovery process. We were asking them, of the three stages, which was a bit hard for them? Many of them talked of the mourning, especially the men. The mountain men are not allowed to mourn. They should stand like a man. If you shed tears, people take it as a weakness. We told them in mourning, crying is not a weakness; it is a strength. It brings you back from where you were.

"And then they shared that the remembrance was a bit hard for them because it took them back to what they went through. It brought back some pictures in their minds, what they saw, what happened. It was like the wound was opened again, like a fresh wound. When it came to the recovery, they said that it is taking time. It is a gradual process. You cannot do this today, wake up tomorrow, and say that you are healed. It is a process that needs time.

Eunice Okwemba
at Mt. Elgon

"The opening up, the sharing was hard, too. They believe as a Kalenjin man you don't need to tell people your problems. If you have a problem you die with it. When you share a problem, then it is a weakness. Who is this person you are sharing with? What level of trust are you putting in this person? That is what they are trying to work on because in their culture, men don't talk about their problems. If they are angry, they just hit. They don't talk.

"And the women were not given the opportunity to speak out. Mostly they are called children. When someone comes to the home and the man is at the front door and asks who is in the home, he will always say, 'No one, only the kids in the kitchen.' He is talking of the kids in the kitchen and the wife is among them. He doesn't say it is my wife and the children, he says just children. So I was asking him, 'Why do you call your wives children? Do they deserve this title?' He said, 'Of course, women are children.' So I said, 'I'm a child? I'm a mother to my children. So, if you call me a child, what do my children call me?' He answered, 'That is not something that we need to negotiate. It is there.' And I responded, 'I respect your culture.'

"Then we asked what the programme has done since we left this place and there were some testimonies from different people. Many people were sharing, saying how we wish that this programme would come again because it came when we really needed it. And we still need it and for those people who are not with us. We have got this group of perpetrators, some of them were in the workshop with us. They asked, 'What of our other friends who have not yet been reached?'

"So we told them that this is not the end. We have just come and we shall still come. Their request was that organization come back to Mt. Elgon and give the teachings, especially in the interior parts like Kubura. That is where the violence really affected everybody. That is where people were being killed and thrown in the forest because it is near the forest.

"There was a lady who was wondering how will she cope? She was just returning back to the community. They had all gone into exile and are now coming back. How do I cope with this person who killed my mother, killed my brother, killed my husband. And here we are sharing the same environment. How do I forgive? Can you really forgive the person who killed your brother, your mother, your husband? She came out and said she is now comfortable. She is now talking to them, despite what happened.

"The issue here was how do I approach this person to tell him this is what I am going through because of what you did? This is the question they were asking. It is hard to have the courage to go and face them. We told them that through the teachings if both sides get the knowledge, you will have the potential for even apologizing to this person who did wrong to you.

"There was a man that very recently lost his brother. The brother had two wives. The first wife had sons and the second wife had only daughters. The elder family took advantage of their step-mother who didn't have sons. They wanted to snatch the land from her because she didn't have sons. He had to use what he had learned. He sat them down and resolved that violence. He was really appreciating this, because if he had not gotten this knowledge, he would not have been able to handle that situation because it was really bad. He was an elderly man, around 70 years." (Eunice Okwemka)

On March 1 2012, FCPT held a community celebration for the group of facilitators who had completed the HROC workshops. They have no electricity, but they use a solar panel and a car battery to power a loudspeaker. The event began outside with a prayer and hymn by a choir. Then a drama demonstrated the process and value of HROC. At that point it began to rain, so the group moved inside.

The celebration continued with testimonies from three of the participants about how HROC had changed their lives. All of the trained facilitators were challenged to sign a commitment to continue to apply HROC to their lives. The commitment forms were given out African style, with everyone singing and dancing to the front. Four beautifully decorated cakes were served.

Community celebration at Kubura on Mt. Elgon. This photo shows the assembled crowd and the mountain landscape.

Getry Agizah (*left*), Gladys Kamonya, Eunice Okwemba (*her back*), Peter Serete (*right*), and Joseph Mamai Makokha (*background*) at the community celebration at Kubura on Mt. Elgon. Although the community has no electricity, they used a solar panel and a car battery to power a loudspeaker.

FCPT Coordinator Getry Agizah addresses the group after moving inside.

Kericho

The District Commissioner asked FPCD for help in Kericho, so they invited all the government officials, District Officers, all the Pastors, all the leaders for two different two-day workshops, matching 15 Kisii with 15 Kalenjins in each workshop. Malesi Kinaro describes:

"We took the first morning just for listening, asking everyone to tell each other how it has been for you during this time. There was a lot of pain expressed. We found even among the Kalenjins there were a lot of losses. They felt the government was not on their side. When we processed the listening exercise, someone said, 'he has gone through what I have just gone through.'

"We took them through all of it, including mediation, because they were leaders and they needed those skills to help their community. But then they told us, 'OK, you have told us what you have told us, but what about the young people. They are the ones who are causing chaos, so you must reach them.'

"So, we began this one-day listening exercise with Kalenjin and Kisii youth. We told the chiefs they had to bring their youth, so the Kisii chief came with his youth and the Kalenjin chief came with his for this one-day listening exercise.

One day we went to Sotik in the interior that was crazy. The Kalenjin chiefs said, 'We have heard that Kisiis are ready to kill us, so we can't do anything.' So it was very tense. We gathered, but we began late. But in the end, I felt that was very effective because they made plans, saying, 'We must re-open the market. Why are we suffering? The Kalenjins are saying they can't sell their animals. Nobody wants to buy them. The Kisiis are saying they can't sell their crops. Why are we hurting each other? On such and such a day we will open this market."

We were the only ones working in this area. There was nobody else. We did a lot of work. If you would go there today, they would tell you, 'if it wasn't for Friends in Peace...'

Rongai

In 2009 FPCD worked with people who were still in IDP camps in Nakuru County. Malesi Kinaro describes that work:

"In Rongai, in Nakuru Country, there was still a lot of hostility, a lot of bitterness, and so FCPD went there. We were just doing HROC because people stayed very, very traumatized. We brought the Kikuyus and the Kalenjins together and did HROC workshops in all locations of the Rongai Constituency.

"In HROC there is an exercise where you talk about somebody you trust. But they were saying, 'I trust nobody. Maybe my wife just a little bit.' 'I don't trust anybody, even my husband I don't trust him. I told him we should go away and he said no, that no one could hurt him there.' For me that was really frightening.

"We did the trust walk and helped them come together. I am a Luhya and the other two facilitators were a Kikuyu and a Kalenjin. People said, "You people look like you really love each other, so it is possible." So it was partly our make-up itself that brought the message. It healed their community. The first impact was that people went back to their farms. That you could see."(Malesi Kinaro)

Reflecting on Peace Process

After FCPT and other Friends had been involved in the trauma healing and reconciliation work for several months, CAPI organized a Reflecting on Peace Process (RPP) workshop with Peter Woodrow from CDA Collaborative Learning Projects in Massachusetts. The RPP workshop that was held at Mabanga in October of 2008 gave the participants an opportunity to step back and analyse the work they had been doing to see what direction they should pursue.

Eden Grace describes the workshop. "The RPP was a very, very useful workshop. We had come to the end of one phase of work and in order to launch the next piece of work we needed to know more about the context in which we were working. Out of that we developed the house to house survey."

Reflecting on Peace Process workshop leader Peter Woodrow discusses intricacies of the peace process

Working at the Reflecting on Peace Process Workshop

Participants in the Reflecting on Peace Process Workshop

Turbo Survey

One of the many outcomes of the RPP workshop was the Turbo Survey. The survey questions that were asked included:

1) How were you and your family personally effected during the post-election violence?

2) What do you feel you lost in the post-election violence (materially or emotionally)?

3) Have you personally encountered any open hostility towards yourself since the IDPs returned? If yes, give an example.

4) Now that the IDPs are mostly resettled, do you imagine the relationship between the communities will get better, get worse, or stay the same? Why?

5) Now that there is "peace" in the community, what do you think could happen in future to disturb the peace?

6) Are you or any of your family members suffering emotional aftereffects from the post-election violence?

7) What are your family's most pressing needs right now? (material, spiritual, psychological)

8) How do you feel about the material assistance that has been provided to people since the post-election violence?

9) What kinds of practical activities do you think would improve relationships between the communities?

10) What role are religious groups playing in rebuilding the community? What would you like them to be doing?

11) Is there anything else you would like to say?

Eden Grace said that, "the survey had all kinds of unintended impacts. We launched into it as a tool for programme planning. It was such an intense piece of work. During the last week in November, 2008, we stayed at Spring Park Motel and visited 634 houses in Turbo in six days.

"We discovered things about militias, small arms, the role of politicians. We found out things that we didn't expect to find out and didn't know what to do with. We felt a

(*above and below*) Members of the FPCT Turbo Survey Team

responsibility. The report on the survey was hand-delivered to the government officials in the area. They said it was very important and it would go up the chain, but they squashed it.

"When we realized the report had not been passed on as agreed, we decided we had to put something in the newspaper, so we paid for an ad, which was a distillation of the report. It was published January 29th, 2009. The local officials who had squashed the report were furious. We were ordered to publish a retraction or we would not be allowed to work in the area. We were not clear to retract what we had said, so we were kicked out of Turbo. Then those officials were transferred and when new officials came in, we were invited back." (Eden Grace)

Here are some excerpts from the survey report:

"Let it not happen again"
A Public Statement by the Friends Church Peace Team on threats of renewed violence in Turbo Division

Summary

In November 2008, the Friends Church Peace Team carried out an intensive survey of Turbo Division, and discovered alarming signs that violence may recur in the near future, particularly in response to the so-called Waki Report. In the public interest, the Friends Church Peace Team draws this matter to the attention of all Kenyans. Urgent action is required to address this threatening situation, to prevent renewed violence in Kenya. ...

Description of interview project

In order to design its future programming, the Friends Church Peace Team carried out a series of interviews in Turbo Division during the week of 23-30 November 2008. Thirty-four (34) team members moved house-to-house in pairs, interviewing a wide spectrum of residents about their current situation, in order to assess the state of "peace" in the community. A total of 634 interviews were conducted. ...

Although the original purpose of the interview project was for the Team's internal planning, it soon became clear that the findings were of time-critical public interest. The Team is therefore releasing this report, even as it continues to analyse the data collected. ...

Urgent Key Findings

Although the interviews contain much interesting data which is yet to be analysed, the Friends Church Peace Team feels an urgent need to bring to the public attention the following findings:

- There is a very widespread opinion that the so-called Waki Report will trigger a new cycle of violence in the very near future.

- There is credible evidence that concrete plans are being made for such violence, with Luhyas and Luos as the particular targets, and local political leaders' involvement.

- The vast majority of the population does not support calls for violence and are feeling very afraid.

- There is an almost total absence of peace-making activity in the Division, either from the churches or from any other organization. ...

Recommendations

The Waki report must be handled with sensitivity. There is a very high probability that it will provoke renewed violence unless the leadership of the country takes active steps to insure that the process is conducted with transparency, maturity, and a lack of inflammatory rhetoric.

The people of Turbo Division need urgent peace-building activities in order to prevent violence in the near future. It is probable that other areas of the country are similarly volatile, although this research was restricted to one Division. The Friends Church Peace Team will continue to work in this area, and urges other organizations to become involved.

The absence of violence in most of the country does not signify that Kenyans are living in peace. The post-election violence of 2007-2008 revealed long-standing and deep-seated problems in Kenyan society which must be meaningfully resolved in order to prevent renewed violence triggered by future events, particularly future elections. Although the events of early 2008 were horrible, they offer Kenyans a unique opportunity to re-forge a national consensus on shared values and social norms, and to create a peaceful future for the country. Let us not waste this opportunity. (FCPT Report on Turbo Survey)

Turbo Interfaith Group

FCPT realized that the work in Turbo needed to be expanded to include all the other religious groups, so they called a meeting and 90 people came. A steering committee was appointed by that group, which included representatives of 16 different Christian churches, and two Muslim mosques. This group planned the Peace Days on the 21st of September, International Day of Peace, holding a Peace Walk in 2010 and 2011.

The Turbo Interfaith Group sponsored intervisitation between different faith groups. Six youth from three churches, the Anglican Church of Kenya, Deliverance Church, and Presbyterian Church, visited the Turbo Mosque. It was the first time any Christians had visited the mosque.

AVP Helps Facilitators in their Own Lives

Benter Obonyo: "I do AVP part time, but it is part of me. Right now I work with orphans and vulnerable children and because of the skills I have gained in AVP, it is not only helping me, but it is also helping the people in the community. Sometimes my patients are HIV-positive; they are vulnerable. Some don't have food; some have been chased away from their home because of their status. Because of the skills that I have gained, I talk to them; I encourage them. They think it is good for them. Sometimes I go home and I find that in our family there is conflict. I talk to them. I encourage them. I say, 'there other ways you can solve your problem.'

"AVP has really helped my life. Some time back I used to be so emotional. I used to get angry over something small. But now it has really helped me to live with people. It has helped me to control my emotions, to have that confidence to tell you when you have wronged me, 'the way you did this and this, I wasn't happy.' It has given me that courage. Before I did AVP, I would not have had that courage to face somebody." (Benter Obonyo, AVP Facilitator)

Eunice Okwemba: "I think God has this purpose for me. When I was called into peace work, I felt like I didn't have any future. I didn't have a job. My children needed to go to school.

International Day of Peace celebrations organized by the Turbo
Interfaith Group Peace Walk 2010 (*above*) and 2011 (*below*)

Why should my children not go to school when I myself went to school? What kind of mother would I be? Those questions were really haunting me.

"I was called for a workshop in Nairobi, a basic AVP. I had never heard about AVP. I wondered, 'do these people really know what they are talking about?' The sharings that were coming out were so touching. Is this what they are talking about? I'm one of those people who could not open up. Before AVP, even if I had a problem, I would keep it to myself. When my sisters were sharing, they would ask me, "you don't have anything you want to say?" I would just say I was alright, but in a real sense I was not alright. In fact, I was at my worst.

"When I started going for apprentice workshops, I thought, "Now I am there! Now I can share." I started slowly by slowly until now I don't have any secrets. If there is something that is burning me, I just talk. I don't quarrel. I just say I am feeling this. Since I started sharing I learned that by sharing you get so much. You heal so fast. Sharing is the most important medicine ever. It's a drug that doesn't have many requirements." (Eunice Okwemba, AVP and HROC Facilitator)

Effectiveness of AVP/HROC

While there are no statistics to measure the effectiveness of the AVP and HROC work that Friends have done, there are many testimonials. Here are but a few of them.

Malesi Kinaro: "I feel that the impact of this organization, Friends in Peace and Community Development, has been very powerful. If you go to Rongai, they will tell you the only organization they have seen there has been Friends in Peace."

Ann Mbugua: "When this problem started, they came to the IDP camp and started this programme of peace. I saw that it helped me very much because I didn't have a good heart with those people. But when I did the basic and the advanced workshops, I was transformed. I was ready to forgive and forget the past. It was very painful, but God is good, because we forgot all those and we are peaceful staying together.

"This AVP work is good because it is helping those people. When we share with them, actually they feel. You can see that feeling from their heart because many of them start to shed tears and they just hug us in a manner that you see that someone is feeling, 'Oh, very good of you to come! Come back to our place. That thing will never come again.'"

Eunice Okwemba: "Mostly the young men participants called me 'Mother', saying, 'you are more than a mother to me. Your teachings are more or less of a real mother.' Whenever I am out in workshops, many young men will come and surround me and ask me questions. I think I have touched many souls; I have healed many souls."

Oliver Kamave was in Lumakanda when the violence started. "I used to be very rough in my business, which was to show videos. I needed money and I would be rough in asking for it, wanting to fight them. The first day of the AVP I thought it was a joke, but then by the second day I was interested to see how it works. I have been an AVP facilitator since  2008. It has changed my life. It has helped me even in my family. If you have a problem with your parents, saying you can't go to a friend's house, it can be a smaller rift but you can talk about it. Now everyone comes to me for advice. I am young. I am not married, but I intervene with my uncles and give them advice on problems in their marriages." (Oliver Kamave, AVP Facilitator)

Frederick Amwoka: "People realized that there is no need for us to keep fighting. We were just trying to make them see the other human beings as a fellow human being. Through the exercises that we conducted at the workshop, people were learning.

"I remember an incident where a woman confessed that she had received Jesus Christ through the workshop. That was amazing; to me it was an achievement. We did not go there to preach; neither did we carry a Bible. But at the end it was a strong testimony that lady gave and we feel it was an impact.

"AVP is different because we were giving them practical skills and not just a lecture. After an AVP workshop, one participant commented, 'We are the real peacemakers in the community now that we are empowered. Other people leading peace initiatives should learn these skills that we have.'

"Even here at Friends Theological Centre sometimes there are conflicts. All the pastors have been trained in AVP. I was at Kitale visiting a former student who was a pastor there. He took me visiting to a house where there was some conflict and I saw him applying very well some AVP techniques. By the time we left there was peace in the house. AVP can help to solve any situation, but it is not a formula. It depends upon our creativity.

"AVP is not a religious programme, but it touches on the spirit of every individual, whatever that spirit is that connects you to your belief or your creator, maybe God, or even ancestors, that is the spirit we touch with the activities and exercises during a workshop. I like the fact that we have a facilitator who is a Muslim. The one thing I like about AVP is that the more you get into it, the more you are learning about ways to resolve conflict. You are always learning.

"All human beings have conflict. Very few people have peace in their heart, so our aim is to let communities stay peaceful. If that is achieved, we will say AVP has matured. Conflict is part and parcel of being human. We just need to get a positive resolution. If that is achieved, that is our joy. If there is anything I enjoy doing, AVP is it." (Frederick Amwoka, Librarian, Friend Theological College)

Cornelius Ambiah: "In Kuresoi, one hour from here, south of Nakuru, we did a workshop bringing people together after the post-election violence to get people talking. I had never been to an AVP workshop where people cried. In this one many people cried. I also had never been to a workshop where people asked forgiveness. In this one it happened. People were so open with one another. Initially when we came in, they even came with Bibles, thinking we would make some references from the scriptures. But AVP is not about references from the scriptures. It is about skills and learning from one another.

"I remember this lady saying 'I have really learned a lot from this workshop, but I cannot leave this workshop until I talk to so and so because she is my neighbour. Being my neighbour, we have lived with her for a very long time, but during post-election violence, her children turned against me, threw me out of my home, and took everything that I had. Although I have gone back, we don't even talk. I just want to tell her I have forgiven her. I am ready and willing to forgive her.'

"So, we had to stop the workshop. It was like an event. It was so moving. We sat in a circle with them in the middle. They embraced each other. I saw true forgiveness. True forgiveness for me is when someone owns up to what they did. 'I did this to you. I am very sorry; I regret my actions. I hope we can still find another way for us to live together as human beings, united by humanity, same spirit, the workmanship of God.'

"I saw true forgiveness, true love. I saw people who had been duped by their political differences. I saw people realizing that we need each other. I saw people who had undergone a lot of pain and then they thought it is time to say good-bye to this pain so that we can set out to live together again as brothers and sisters, as families, as neighbours, as communities, and probably as tribes, and maybe one community which is Kenya. It was so moving, so outstanding." (Cornelius Ambiah, AVP Facilitator)

AVP and HROC Work Continues

Getry Agizah became the Coordinator for FCPT in June, 2010. "As I have been embarking on this journey, working with the youth in Turbo, it might be a drop of blood in the ocean, but to me that drop is so strong. It is a blessing I am counting. We have touched lives. At FCPT we did it without using the Bible, but we used a transformational message to make human beings realize their potential.

"I don't know how much I can take credit. AGLI, FPCD, FCPT, all these organizations deal in that transforming power. They have done a tremendous job. One of the participants said to me, 'I know that you are not a pastor, but you have taken me to heaven, made me what I am.'

"It is one thing that makes me see tomorrow, one thing that encourages me to keep on being peaceful. I am happy being the Coordinator. I never want to be a pastor; I never want to be in the media. Interacting with me these people want to share." (Getry Agizah, FCPT Coordinator)

FCPT and FPCD in western Kenya, and CAPI and the AVP-Trust in Nairobi, continue the AVP and HROC work as funds allow. Friends are also investing in the long-term with the peace curriculum, which is the subject of the next chapter.

Chapter Seven
Peace Curriculum: Friends Investment in the Future

At the Kenya National Quaker Peace Conference in January of 2008, the 65 Friends gathered there thought beyond the immediate humanitarian and trauma healing needs into the longer term. The youth are the future, so they set up a committee chaired by Kakamega Yearly Meeting Secretary General Wesley Sasita to develop a peace curriculum. He describes how that work started:

"We had a mandate from the FCPT. We called a meeting of all the heads of schools and deliberated over these issues. The Principals said a peace curriculum was very timely. Besides the post-election violence, we needed to work on discipline in the schools. We called on the Education Section of Kakamega Yearly Meeting and of other yearly meetings to advise us on how to put a curriculum in place. Henry Mkutu of Bware Yearly Meeting, Kisii, was involved. Then we started working. We called upon our teachers to see who could work on writing curriculum. Fortunately we had members who participated in curriculum writing at the ministry level, so we could pick those who were in our schools to be on the committee."

FUM Director of Africa Ministries John Muhanji took on the peace curriculum as a call, as he explains:

"Since the Quakers in Kenya are a big team, my prayer is that all Kenyan Quakers will be brought into an understanding of a peace-building process, so that everybody understands from the child to the adult what it means to be a Quaker, what it means to be a peace-builder, what it means to create an environment of peace wherever you are. If peace is strongly advocated among the churches, the pastors, the leaders, then it will sink into their communities and they will start to practice peace wherever they are.

"That was the initial reason for starting the peace curriculum. We have not inculcated a culture of peace in our approach to issues as Quakers. The people where you can transform a culture are the young people. You can't change my culture at this time. It is not possible. I will remain as an old person.

"But we can inculcate a culture of peace in young people, and once they grow up, it will already be getting deeper in them. When they come into the community, when they reach my age, they will be speaking nothing else but peace. They will understand the concept of peace. They will know what it means to be peaceful.

"That can be done through the education process. Education is the learning process where we change the attitudes of people. You cannot change my attitudes, but the attitudes of people can be created in schools. Children learn new things and adopt new approaches in schools. That is why this curriculum was a call that I have taken on as an instrument for peace.

"This not only addresses all the Quaker churches, but everybody in the Quaker schools and the Quaker schools have everybody, irrespective of religion. Therefore, we are reaching everybody. The government has given us an opportunity to air our heritage that had been buried in Quaker history. But it can be made live today and in the future through the generations in the schools.

"These children now have experienced violence. Because they have experienced violence, this curriculum touches them and reminds them what they need to be doing, and how they need to prevent violence rather than reacting. The violence was mostly done by the young people and to them it was a joy. They felt energized to throw stones as they were running up and down. You only need to do one thing, give them beer, give them drugs, charge them, and they are on their own. But once they understand their rights and the importance of human life, they can be empowered."

True to this call, John Muhanji gave such inspiring presentations during a 2009 fund-raising trip to the U.S. that he not only raised considerable funds for the peace curriculum, but also recruited two different groups to help in writing the curriculum, the Education Department of George Fox University in Oregon and the United Society of Friends Women in Iowa. The George Fox University group worked on the secondary curriculum and Charlotte Strangland is currently working on the primary curriculum.

The George Fox University group worked with Kenyan educators to produce the secondary curriculum entitled *A Curriculum for Peace and Conflict Management,* a collaborative project between FUM-African Ministries, Friends Secondary Schools, Kenya, and George Fox University, USA. Educators from George Fox University came to Kenya and worked with Kenyan educators, who eagerly developed a very creative curriculum. Twenty-five teachers from Friends Schools in Kenya were involved, along with eleven members of the George Fox University Peace Curriculum Committee, which was chaired by Eloise Hockett.

The published curriculum was printed with financial support from Philadelphia Yearly Meeting and consists of three documents: *Syllabus, Teacher's Guide* with suggested references and activities, and *Resource Guide* with a section for each lesson written by Kenyan educators.

Peace Curriculum Rationale

Conflict is universal. Can anything be done about it? Could these conflicts have been prevented? Is there a way forward? What is the role of the church? What is the best form of intervention? How should the intervention be carried out? Conflict resolution is needed at all levels of society. It is hoped that the Peace and Conflict Management curriculum developed under the guidance of the Friends Churches in Kenya will prepare Kenyan students to be responsible citizens and promoters of peace throughout Kenya and the world.

This curriculum begins with the Kenya National Anthem and how it promotes peace, especially verse three:

Natujenge taifa letu	Let all with one accord
Ee, ndio wajibu wetu	In common bond united,
Kenya istahili heshima	Build this our nation together
Tuungane mikono	And the glory of Kenya
Pamoja kazini	The fruit of our labour
Kila siku tuwe na shukrani	Fill every heart with thanksgiving

John Muhanji talks about the Syllabus, which is shown below:

"The first 'Who am I?' section addresses a strong element of each person, so that when you understand who you are, then you understand the other person. The concept of Adam looking at who he is, and looking at all the others from your image, it takes you back to the origin of creation, and makes you appreciate one another in the same image that you see

---

Syllabus
1) Introduction
2) Who Am I? (3 lessons)—Joseph Simiya Muhindi
3) Peace (7 lessons)—Eunice Kanaga Majanga
4) Virtues that Promote Peace (4 lessons)—Elizabeth Amadi
5) Conflict and Conflict Management (7 lessons)—Hellen Anyanga
6) Life Skills (4 lessons)—Elizabeth Amadi
7) Human Rights and Responsibilities (5 lessons)—Zadock Malesi
8) Peace and Health (4 lessons)—Mr. Kitui
9) Peace and Environment (7 lessons)—Amos Wanjala

yourself. You see yourself in the other person. When I see myself in you, I feel bad in hurting you, because I see I am hurting myself." (John Muhanji)

A Curriculum for Peace and Conflict Management has been piloted in several secondary schools in Kenya and teachers have been trained in its use. It has already been accepted by the Kenya Institute of Education accreditation process for use in all secondary schools in the country. It is currently being used quite successfully in most Friends schools with the hope that other schools will pick it up soon.

John Muhanji describes the bright future of this programme: "The peace curriculum itself is a powerful tool. As the Friends Church Peace Team, AVP, and other groups work on trying to train people in the communities, the schools are trying to train the young people. The young people will grow up and become part of the communities, so these programmes are married together to create communities of peace. The children in the schools and the people in the society are in this process together.

"One of the key issues is how do we insure there is proper monitoring and evaluation of this programme in the schools? How do we make sure this programme is fully being taught and how do we make sure it makes sense to young people? What kind of activities should we design to make sure that children participate in this peace process? Who will take the responsibility of monitoring and evaluation and how will we finance such a person?

"We have been having some trainings for the teachers. We brought the Principals on board before this curriculum was put in place. Every year we have meetings of the Principals. We wanted them to buy into the programme and they did. They are the ones who insisted that we need someone to help with monitoring and evaluation of this new curriculum.

"So, we started discussing having an Education Superintendent of Schools in the FUM office. One of the major assignments in their job description will be the monitoring and evaluation of the peace curriculum. Now we are raising the funds and we are almost ready to engage this person.

"We have a project to support the peace curriculum called 'SEEDS, Seeds Educating Every Deserving Student'. Friends from Iowa Yearly Meeting agreed to give us capital to start this project of growing seed corn. We leased 100 acres of land last year, grew seed corn, harvested, and got some good profit. That money from the seed corn is going into the curriculum project, so we are not going out asking people to give us money to run these workshops.

"So, the systems are all orderly in the Quaker schools to enhance good performance and a quality education. Once we have good performance and a quality education, the peace curriculum will be a call and everybody will be looking forward to taking their child to a Quaker school that has those values." (John Muhanji)

The peace curriculum is an investment in the long-tern future, but what of the near-term? The next Kenya election is scheduled for either late 2012 or early 2013. Is the country prepared to prevent further violence? Has the trauma from the previous violence been healed? What reforms are in place in the new Constitution? What are Friends doing to prepare? These questions are addressed in the next chapter.

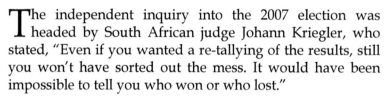

CHAPTER EIGHT
The Way Forward
Independent Inquiries / International Criminal Court

The independent inquiry into the 2007 election was headed by South African judge Johann Kriegler, who stated, "Even if you wanted a re-tallying of the results, still you won't have sorted out the mess. It would have been impossible to tell you who won or who lost."

The report presented in September, 2008, indicated that there were widespread irregularities, including bribery, intimidation, vote-buying, and problems in tallying of the results. Even worse, the report found that election officials felt that they could tamper with the results with impunity.

The inquiry into the causes of the violence, headed by Kenyan judge Philip Waki, produced a comprehensive report and a sealed envelope was handed to Kofi Annan with names of senior level politicians and influential people implicated in the violence. Kofi Annan had chaired the African delegation that brokered the solution to the 2007 election crisis. International Criminal Court (ICC) Prosecutor Luis Moreno-Ocampo expressed interest in investigating the Kenya post-election violence and Kenya was given a year beginning July, 2009, to establish a tribunal to investigate crimes against humanity associated with the post-election violence. When the Kenya Parliament voted down the establishment of a tribunal, Kofi Annan gave the sealed envelope to the ICC prosecutor who took up the matter and presented cases against six individuals, three each in two cases, to the three-judge Pretrial ICC panel to determine if charges would be confirmed to proceed to trial.

On 23rd January 2012, the charges were confirmed for four of the suspects, two in each of the cases. On the PNU side, Deputy Prime Minister and Finance Minister Uhuru Kenyatta and Head of Public Service Francis Muthaura were charged. Three days later both resigned their administrative positions, but Kenyatta kept the Deputy Prime Minister position because it was said to be political and not government. Charges were not issued against Postmaster General Hussein Ali, who was the head of the police at the time of the violence, saying that the evidence that police participated in the violence was not strong enough.

On the ODM side charges were issued against William Ruto, Member of Parliament from the Rift Valley Eldoret North area, and radio presenter Joshua Sang. Charges were not issued for Henry Kosgey, Member of Parliament from Tinderet. The court emphasized that the suspects were merely charged, but considered innocent until proven guilty, and that the Prosecutor could still enter other evidence against the two who were not charged that would strengthen those cases. Both Kenyatta and Ruto are contenders for President in the 2012 (or 2013) election and neither has withdrawn their candidacy.

There was great concern that violence would accompany this ICC announcement. From every corner, politicians, civil society, and churches, came calls for calm. Security forces were very visible in potentially hot spot areas. David Zarembka set up a call-in network which 45 citizen reporters joined. Although they reported that all was calm, everyone was clearly being careful. Some shops were not open; market day didn't happen in Jua Kali; and in Turbo police broke up gatherings of youths as they began to form. Some people were saying they did not like the ruling, but they remained calm.

New Constitution (2010)

As a part of the political resolution of the crisis, a constitutional committee of local and international experts was commissioned to draft a new constitution. A draft of the new constitution was presented to the politicians in November 2009. After six months of negotiations, a final draft was published three months before the August 2010 referendum. The new constitution included significant limitations on the powers of the president, by making the legislative and judiciary branches of government, and the Electoral Commission independent. Control over local issues will be transferred to the new county governments. It represented a compromise between the desires of some of the PNU parties for a strong, centralized government and those of the ODM for more independence of the regional governments and limits to powers of the president.

Both the PNU and the ODM supported the new constitution. The main political opposition to the new constitution was led by William Ruto, Member of Parliament from Eldoret in the Rift Valley. He was joined by the National Council of Churches of Kenya, including some of the leadership of Friends Churches, because they objected to two provisions: for abortion in very limited circumstances and for Islamic family courts. But most Friends voted for the constitution and it passed with more than two-thirds of the votes in a peaceful referendum.

The new constitution provides for a new structure of the legislative branch, including a Senate and a House, as well as representatives for the handicapped, youth, and women. The eight provinces with their 208 constituencies were abolished and instead 47 counties were established with 280 constituencies. The Independent Electoral Boundaries Commission released their report on the new boundaries for all constituencies, and gave 60 days for comments during which hearings were held in all districts. At the hearings there was some fighting and people were injured.

Devolution of the government, decentralization of power to the new counties, is also an important reform in the new constitution. In addition to the national representatives Kenyans will be voting for county officers: Governor, Deputy Governor, and County Councillor.

John Muhanji discusses the process of change in Kenya: "For a country that has rooted itself in corruption within every sector, it will take time to root it out. Sometimes the person who is carrying out the weeding is the person practicing the corruption. As you weed others, without knowing, you leave the main culprit. It is not possible to close up the whole institution to zero and start recruiting afresh, so this element will be there. But as we continue with a strong constitution and continue to draw people into the systems, we will see people changing the approach to issues.

"With these challenges Kenya is really ready to embrace a lot of big changes. Other countries in the region are not yet ready for that process. They are still many years back. Our constitution is the only one like it in Africa. That is why we are trying to see how it will work. If it works well, we will have a sound nation.

"That is our prayer, that God may help us to see this constitution fully implemented. It will be slow, but will have a big impact. One issue is that they are decentralizing all the governance from one central place to counties. By releasing the powers that have been concentrated in one central place, by giving powers to the various counties, the person at the top no longer has all the powers. The person at the top has the power to unite these counties as one nation, but he or she does not have the consolidated powers as it has been before. The powers are within the counties. The counties become decision-makers about development. Now we are not looking for accountability from the central government, but from the counties. Changes will begin down there.

"To start implementing to the letter will change people's attitudes. One of the ways we are helping to implement this constitution is through the peace curriculum. These young people are the ones going to the colleges and will end up in the government positions. They will have peace in mind as they approach the future of Kenya." (John Muhanji)

As the first book in this series went to print in March 2012, the election date had not been settled, but the Presidential candidates were already campaigning, even the two who are facing charges in the ICC.

Friends Prepare for the Next Election

Friends are hard at work to prevent violence in the next election, as far as funds allow. While donations poured in during the post-election crisis period, it is harder to raise funds for violence prevention. However, the AVP, HROC and other peace and reconciliation work is accomplished as efficiently as possible. In contrast to other organizations, there is no "sitting allowance" paid to participants. Larger NGOs pay participants to come to their workshops and that is how they get a crowd. But then the participants are there merely to get paid and care little for the information. When Friends first go into a community they have to explain they will not give a sitting allowance. Some refuse to participate, but those who do generally become very committed to the work.

From each basic workshop many of the participants go on to the advanced training and then training of trainers (ToT). Those who complete ToT are apprentices in several workshops and then become facilitators who spread the peace work in their communities.

"We don't go to Kisii any more because people there are trained. The current funding we have now, we just call their coordinator, send the money, and he goes ahead with the workshops. He uses his local facilitators and they do AVP, so it is very cost effective." (Malesi Kinaro)

Civic Education

Friends are clear that in the lead-up to the next election, civic education is a great need. Kenyans generally do not understand the new constitution and many will say they depend upon their leaders to read and interpret it for them. That means they do not understand their rights and will resort to violence instead of using the provisions of the Constitution and the laws implementing it. In the next election, instead of only voting for the President and their Member of Parliament, they also have to vote for a Senator, a women Senator, and county officials.

Nairobi

Nairobi Yearly Meeting in collaboration with CAPI held a meeting of their pastors on February 6, 2012, to prepare for the next election. The keynote speaker was Nancy Abisaí, a Friend who was on the Constitutional Commission that drafted the new Constitution and several other commissions implementing various reforms, such as, land reforms, women's issues, and environmental issues. She explained the process for implementing the Constitution requires a series of new laws and, at that time, hearings were in process for public input into these new laws. She said that even though some Friends pastors had opposed the new Constitution, it is now the law of the land and they must get involved in its implementation and in civic education of their congregations.

Turbo

FCPT held a weekend retreat on February 10th and 11th 2012, to train their AVP facilitators for civic education. At the end of that retreat, Benter Obonyo looked ahead to the next election: "It is difficult to say about the next election. Now, with the work that we have done and will do on the ground in Turbo Division, people will be knowledgeable. Apart from AVP, we have been taught about civic education, about our constitution. It is like before we were blind, we couldn't see

FCPT Turbo Facilitator group meeting at Lugari Yearly Meeting's Lake Basin Headquarters February 11-12 2012

what was in our constitution. Now we have those skills and we can go to our community and talk to them about our constitution, about alternatives to violence. I believe that this time, the elections will be peaceful because our leaders are not going to drag people the way they used to because now people are knowledgeable. They have to convince us to choose someone, not because of their tribe, not because they come from a locality. I believe elections will be good, unless otherwise. But the more we put more effort, not just in Turbo, but in Kenya as a whole, we will have peaceful elections."

Bernard Onjala was also at that FCPT AVP Facilitators Retreat and was inspired:

"I will be doing civic education. Already people are calling me, saying, 'Where are you?' When I go back, my friends who will ask me, 'What did you get from the retreat?' So now we will start going to the community to make them realize that the new constitution works. It's workable and it's friendly to everyone, so long as you can get a person who can interpret it in a local language, fairly, without misdirecting anyone, I think the people will make a good choice. It is our responsibility to defend the local citizen to go out and work with the community and make them realize this thing is ours; it is our voice. The constitution is our voice and our mind." (Bernard Onjala)

Turning the Tide

A new programme in Kenya initiated by the British Quaker Peace and Social Witness, Turning the Tide (TTT) goes a step further than AVP/HROC, and organizes groups to undertake a campaign for change. To begin the programme, TTT drew on those who had already been trained in AVP and HROC in Kenya.

Eunice Okwemba describes her experience with TTT: "CAPI requested the TTT programme to come to Kenya, so Laura Shipley Chico and Steve Whiting came. They picked AVP facilitators to do the TTT workshop. At first there was just a three-day workshop and TTT didn't do anything. Then we did a two-week workshop, and I realized it was really a serious social change programme. We made work plans for clusters. What were we going to work on? Bad governance we took as the issue we wanted to work on. We analysed the pillars of power, and broke down those pillars. Our unity and cohesiveness can break down those pillars. We assembled 20 youth and talked to them about how violence can be solved by nonviolence. We are working with youth because they are the most vulnerable. When there is violence, they are the front line. But they were being overlooked. The Vihiga cluster group went to their District Officer (DO) and said they needed to be represented. They gave him a list of those who would represent them and the DO agreed."

Betty Atieno was hired as TTT's Nairobi Field Officer in 2011. She describes the programme: "While AVP focuses on personal change, TTT engages groups in positive change, challenging social injustices and holding leaders accountable. There are eight constituencies in Nairobi. We merged each two constituencies to make four groups working on different issues. In Makadara and Kamukunji there was great success in creating awareness. There are Youth Devolved Funds to create awareness of the devolution process which is going on in Kenya. They had a one-day road show in these constituencies giving out information on how to access these funds. Some youth groups are already visiting the office to fill out the forms for the funds. Other groups are planning other campaigns. They have had meetings to strategize on campaigns.

"In one community there was a hall built for youth, intended to be for sports, dramas, and other activities so that they don't have to walk so far to the centre of the city. But it was only a shell with no roof, doors or windows. The money was allocated, but had not been used to finish the hall. The TTT group held meetings and identified the problem at a meeting on 20th December. By the end of January they had identified the leaders and figured out how to approach them. Different people were assigned different duties to collect that feedback so they can make a plan.

"TTT is a new concept. Mostly the youth just sit and complain. But these projects make them be clear and give them the courage to go talk to the leaders. Before they wouldn't have had the guts to approach their seniors on an issue affecting them. Now they see the importance of attending community meetings. It used to be just the old folks at these meetings, but now the youth are attending. It gives them a chance to advance their projects. They are coming up and taking steps. When they find out that resources have been allocated for them, but not used for them, they open their eyes and learn their rights. They hold the leaders accountable."

Predictions for the Next Election

Agatha Ganira: "I pray that it will be peaceful next time because if it happens again, it will be more serious. Some people have a fear of going for the election. They are not interested in voting. Last time they lost their children and they gained nothing. They are after justice. They want the trial at the ICC to proceed because no one is listening to them here. But I went for the Peace Walk on the International Day of Peace in September 2011. People do not want war. They do not want war at all. They don't want to see that bloodshed again. And there is friendship. 'That is my friend,' they say. When you look at the way people are relating, they are now working as a team. I think people are not willing to fight again, or follow anyone blindly."

John Muhanji: "Why do we have violence in developing nations? It is not that politicians are driving us to violence. The reason is poverty and oppression. Poverty leads to malnutrition and unemployment. I don't see us becoming a peaceful nation unless we address the poverty and oppression of the people. With the gap between rich and poor continuing to widen, how can we expect to have peace, when some people are enjoying and others are not enjoying."

Hezron Masitsa was also concerned about unemployment: "I had a conversation with two of Kenya's MPs. They said that Friends are doing good work in Kenya, but if we don't address the unemployment problem it is all for naught. If that problem is not addressed, we will continue to have violence in Kenya. There are the masses of idle youth. We deal with their attitudes and address peace and development only on a small scale.

"The educational system is partly to blame. Some time ago there was a change. They abolished the technical institutions, which was a mistake. TTT was asking the youth what they want. They all want diplomas, degrees, and an office job. What are we teaching? Even those with degrees that take office jobs do not have the proper skills to function in those jobs. If they are trained in electrical work or plumbing, there are great needs. As for me, the type of education I received prepared me for an office job. If we invest in practical skills, young people will begin valuing self-employment and hence the creation of wealth. (Hezron Masitsa)

To address issues of poverty and unemployment, FPCD opened the Friends in Peace and Community Development College at the Lubao Friends Peace Centre in January of 2012. They offer vocational training in motor vehicle mechanics, computer systems, tailoring and garment making, carpentry, electrical installation, and masonry.

They have a staff of young people expert in each area who are eager to train youth with life skills that can lead to employment or their own business. Kingsley Kijedi is the computer teacher: "I really want that healing to have brotherhood. I don't want to know where someone comes from, whether he is Kikuyu, Kalenjin, Luo, Luhya, but I see him as a brother. That is why we decided to teach these things. We can teach ourselves; we can have that mental

strength. We went out looking for youths and started giving them those basics.

"I'm proud to be Kenyan. That is why I want to erase those first memories and set in new memories of brotherhood and love. That's why I volunteered to teach my friends how to use computers, and how to do one or two things for this institution, because it is a Peace Centre, a Community Development Peace Centre. You can't have peace just by talking, but you can have peace by doing something together. I want them to know a few things. Once they know how to use the Internet, they can send some beautiful peace messages. Now that we are approaching an election, hopefully this year or next year, we don't want to have what happened. We don't want to see it again, so we can use these computers to send those peace messages, those lovely ones to each other, whether abroad or within the country." (Kingsley Kijedi)

Cornelius Ambiah: "I think what is being done is enough. The ICC is trying to help us and that is a blessing. When Waki was given the job of investigating, he was so wise, which I think was given to him by God. They put in the measures, gave the parliament three months to come up with a tribunal. Parliament refused, so Kofi Annan gave them more time. In the end the envelope with the list was turned over to the ICC and I think they have a lot of wisdom.

"I want to believe that the judicial system has been revamped. I don't believe that Kenya can go back to what happened after the last election.

"I have hope. I look on Facebook and people are saying, "if a big shot from my community comes to me and tells me to kill my neighbour, I will just take the money but not do anything. The youth have formed their own community-based groups and they ask if AVP can come and give them some skills, teach them to be entrepreneurs. I think we are doing a good job, making an impact on the lives of many people. It is my prayer that we have a peaceful election in 2012 or 2013 and into the future of Kenya."

CHAPTER NINE
The 2013 Election

Citizen Reporter/Call-in Center—David Zarembka

After a successful pilot project for the 2010 Burundian elections, which is described in the *Peaceways* Fall 2011 issue, AGLI decided to implement a more ambitious project for the 2013 Kenyan elections.

The concept was to train citizens to become "citizen reporters" and connect them with a Call-in Center where they could text any information they gather in their community. The whole election cycle was observed and not just election day itself since much of the fraud and intimidation occurs before the election, and post-election violence is possible as occurred on a massive scale in Kenya after the December 2007 election.

We conducted thirty-four trainings and enrolled 1,204 citizen reporters in our network. Many of these citizen reporters are in remote places where the media never goes.

The five-hour citizen reporter training sessions were filled with discussion, role play, guidelines for citizen reporters, and security concerns. For example, the citizen reporter needs to be aware of indicators of violence such as hate speech or development of youth gangs. These indicators need to be reported to the Call-in Center so that remedial action can quickly be taken. December 18 was the last day of the month-long voter registration. Peter Serete, the Coordinator for the Call-in Center, texted the 900 citizen reporters that had been trained by then and asked them to go to their polling stations to see if the ending process was orderly and proper for the last two days. Over 200 of the citizen reporters sent in text messages and there were no reports of major problems.

On January 17 most political parties in Kenya had their nominations for the various elective positions. We texted our citizen reporters and asked them to observe these nominations in their community. We got many messages of late delivery of ballot papers, anger at the waiting, and bribery during the nominations. Then the major political campaigning began and the citizen reporters reported numerous cases of bribery by the local politicians and their agents.

There is no point in receiving accurate information if nothing is done about negative situations that are reported. As we developed this programme, I was worried about how we might respond to incidents of intimidation and violence. Our time and energy concentrated on reacting to the information we received.

The most serious reports we received were from Mt. Elgon. From 2006 to 2008 this area had an armed conflict between two clans of the Sabaot in which about 600 people were killed and another 100,000 displaced. We had five citizen reporter trainings on Mt. Elgon for 189 citizen reporters.

One of our Quaker guidelines is to work with all sides in any conflict. This includes the government officials who have little guidance or training on how to resolve the contentious issues that are arising in their communities. Two chiefs and three sub-chiefs, community-level government officials, attended HROC workshops on Mt. Elgon. Getry Agizah, the FCPT coordinator, was asked by a local police commissioner to meet with her police officers. Getry met with 45 officers and could feel the fear inside them. They told her that they wanted the public to understand that they are also human and have feelings.

We had just finished our first workshop there on August 15, when the Call-in Center received a report that one of our original HROC participants in Mt. Elgon had been assassinated in his home. The next morning a few of our HROC facilitators/citizen reporters visited with the grieving wife and asked her if one of them could speak at the funeral. She agreed. We texted our local contacts and about forty of them attended this funeral. Erastus Chesondi, our lead HROC facilitator and citizen reporter on Mt. Elgon, gave a strong peace message at the funeral. We also attended a chief's meeting to discuss this situation and the FCPT/AGLI participants gave their feedback. Soon thereafter four more people were killed, a school was burned down, and hate leaflets were distributed ordering all those who were not born on Mt. Elgon to return to where they came from.

This led us to increase our response in Mt. Elgon. That decision was also made possible by the political situation. In the 2007-2008 post-election violence one of the most contentious conflicts was between the Kikuyu and Kalenjn groups. FCPT/AGLI had put considerable resources into working with the youth of the Turbo area, a hot spot of Kikuyu-Kalenjin conflict. Two presidential candidates in the 2013 election, Uhuru Kenyatta (Kikuyu) and William Ruto (Kalenjin), were on opposite sides of the 2007 election and both are charged and awaiting trial at the International Criminal Court for inciting violence. When they made an alliance in December of 2012 with Kenyatta running for President and Ruto as his running mate, the tension in Turbo was considerably lessened. So, FCPT/AGLI decided to focus their efforts in Mt. Elgon.

Before the end of 2012, FCPT/AGLI had held four HROC workshops for about 80 individuals in Mt. Elgon. In January of 2013 we trained eighteen healing companions (eight women and ten men) from Mt. Elgon at the Peace House at Lugari Yearly Meeting. Theoneste Bizimana from Rwanda and Florence Ntakarutimana from Burundi led this training. Before the election these apprentice facilitators together with lead facilitators conducted eight basic HROC workshops on Mt. Elgon for about 160 people. Kathy and Joe Ossmann, Benter Obonyo, and Ezra Kigondu did an assessment of the work on Mt. Elgon, which is reported in Chapter Ten.

Voter Education—David Zarembka

In August 2010, Kenyans overwhelming approved a new constitution. While there were many changes including enhanced rights for women, the biggest change was that the nine provinces were divided into 47 counties that will have control over local issues. In this devolved government each county will be led by an elected governor and a county-wide legislature.

In order for citizens to understand these changes, FCPT/AGLI conducted 72 one-day seminars for 4,500 participants plus 13 shorter, informal seminars in churches and government meetings for about 1,500 people. These seminars were based on the philosophy that if people know and understand the political process and are willing to participate in it, they are less likely to resort to violence to redress their grievances.

The seminar covered four main topics: (1) the electoral process, (2) the leadership and integrity requirements according to the new constitution, (3) the Bill of Rights, and (4) the new devolved governmental system. The boundaries of the 47 new counties were drawn along ethnic and clan lines in many parts of the country, leading to minority groups with no possibility of winning electoral office with tribal-based voting patterns. The government itself has determined that 27 of the new counties have potential for ethnic violence.

We have found that, on the one hand, citizens know very little about the new constitution, but, on the other hand, they are eager to learn. Most of the seminars had between 40 and 80 participants. People did not want to end the seminar when it was time for the facilitators to return home.

Voter registration for the upcoming election was disappointing and well under the goal set by the Independent Electoral and Boundaries Commission (IEBC). Eighteen million voters were expected to enroll, but only 14 million voters did so. On Mt. Elgon FCPT/AGLI did civic education in three of the six locations, the smallest electoral unit in Kenya. Those three locations with civic education seminars had nine percent higher registration of voters than those where we did not conduct civic education seminars. Voter registration in Turbo constituency where FCPT/AGLI has been working for the last few years was 92 percent of the estimated, 21 percent more than the two adjoining constituencies.

Can we claim credit for this success? Getry Agizah, the FCPT coordinator, thinks so. Of course, the kind of work we do is not like drilling for oil, where it comes gushing out and you can claim success. While during the 2007 election and post-election violence, the youth in Turbo division spearheaded the violence, Getry says "now they are interested, even excited by the election. While they did not register well in 2007, they have this time. If you reach out to the youth, they will respond."

Voter Education Programme—Kathy Ossmann

In mid-February, just weeks before Kenyans cast votes in the first election since adopting a new constitution in 2010, I co-facilitated a voter education session in southern Nandi County, site of significant post-election violence after the last national election in 2007. We met in a church near the cluster of Quaker schools in Kaimosi. Quaker pastors from the Tuloi Friends Yearly Meeting were invited, in keeping with the FCPT/AGLI strategy of training people in positions to share the information with others.

The devolution of the centralized to county government structures significantly changed the electoral procedures. Our voter education curriculum included descriptions of the structures and roles for the new national and county units, responsibilities for each elective office and how these changes impacted the voting process.

The new constitution also addresses many of the problems that led to conflict and violence during and after the 2007 election, including fraudulent voting. For example, the Independent Electoral and Boundaries Commission (IEBC) was created in the new constitution to ensure free, fair and transparent elections.

Our sessions included materials about what to expect at the polling station with this and other changes to prevent fraud. The training also covered the importance of voting, making wise choices, the new Code of Conduct signed by all candidates and political parties, and the "leadership and integrity" portion of the constitution.

At the conclusion, we asked the pastors to share this information with their churches on the three Sundays remaining before the election. All commented that they had learned something new in the session and agreed to pass along the information. About halfway through our session a young man on crutches joined us. He raised some excellent questions about policies for assisting disabled voters during the voting process. I'm quite certain that he, too, intended to share the information with other disabled people in his community.

4th March 2013 Election—David Zarembka

On March 9th Uhuru Kenyatta was declared the 4th president-elect of Kenya by the Chairman of the Independent Electoral and Boundaries Commission (IEBC). It was a close, but not close, contest. Uhuru obtained 6,173,433 votes for 50.06 percent of the votes cast. Raila Odinga received 5,340,548 votes for 43 percent, so it was not close. But the winning candidate must obtain 50 percent plus one vote in order to win. As you can see above, Uhuru only got 0.06 percent or 8418 more votes than he needed for the absolute majority. Otherwise there would have been a run-off election. Upon hearing the announcement, Raila Odinga indicated that he was going to challenge these results in court.

At that time our citizen reporters texting the Call-in Center reported tension in the Raila stronghold areas, but no unrest or violence. One message reported, "Siaya County (Raila's home) is so calm and have received and accepted the final presidential results. Residents are happy for the sake of peace, for economic growth. They say, 'Uhuru is Kenya's 4th President.'"

Urging the country to use the judicial system rather than the streets, Raila Odinga filed a petition with the Supreme Court of Kenya contesting the election. The petition argued that there were enough irregularities that could give Odinga more than 8,418 votes, which would have thrown the election into a run-off. The Supreme Court had until the end of March to issue a ruling and the whole country waited.

On March 30, the Kenya Supreme Court ruled that Uhuru Kenyatta and William Ruto had been elected president and deputy president. Raila Odinga conceded defeat; on April 9th Kenyatta anad Ruto were sworn in; and the country remained peaceful.

Kenya 2013 Election Observation—Kathy Ossmann

African Great Lakes Initiative (AGLI) and Friends Church Peace Teams (FCPT) were among several organizations which were accredited by the IEBC to observe Kenya's national election on March 4, 2013. Others included the Carter Center, the European Union, the African Union, the National Council of Churches in Kenya, Quaker Peace Network-Africa, Turning the Tide, and a consortium of Kenyan civil society called Elections Observation Group.

Election observation was part of a AGLI/FCPT peace building strategy to prevent election violence, which focused on areas of western Kenya that had experienced violence in 2008 and, because of diverse ethnic populations, were susceptible to recurring violence in 2013. These included Turbo Constituency in Uasin Gishu County, Mount Elgon Constituency in Bungoma County, Vihiga Constituency in Vihiga County, and several constituencies in both Nandi and Kakamega counties. One location in Nyanza County was also included, not because of possible violence, but simply because we have a long-time lead facilitator who lives there.

AGLI/FCPT submitted names of 265 observers who were accredited by the IEBC. In day-long sessions observers were trained on the Code of Conduct for aspirants and political parties; processes for voting, counting and tallying; information in the "Guidelines and Code of Ethics" booklet IEBC provided for observers; and procedures for documenting and reporting observations. Upon completion of the sessions, 259 trainees received their IEBC badges and FCPT t-shirts and caps to wear for identification on election day.

Unlike other observer groups, AGLI/FCPT used a grass-roots approach. Except for three international observers, all volunteers were Kenyans living in the focus areas. Wherever possible, observers were assigned to the polling station in which they had registered. This allowed them to vote and also meant that they were familiar with the IEBC clerks, agents and voters in that location. When we had enough in a single location, pairs of observers worked each stream at the polling station. Also contrary to other observer groups, AGLI/FCPT observers were not paid an allowance or provided with meals. This was possible since they were in polling stations near their homes and it ensured a high level of commitment to the process. A total of 104 completed observation forms were turned in from 112 observers who worked in 83 polling station/streams.

Additionally, 1,030 trained community reporters observed the areas outside of polling stations and throughout their communities. They reported to the Call-in Center (CIC) via SMS text messages. The CIC had been in use since we initiated citizen reporting in mid-2012. A total of 53 messages pertaining to the election came into the CIC. Our CIC Coordinator managed these messages using SMSFrontline software which allowed us to keep the identity of the reporter confidential. This choice was made out of a concern for the safety of our community reporters. Consequently, unless the reporter included their location in a message, it is not possible to correlate every message with a polling station.

Our election observers reported that the conduct of the election varied considerably from station to station. In 19 of 83 (23%) polling stations there were no problems reported. Additionally, 21 of 53 SMS messages received by the CIC indicated no problems in and around polling stations. Of these SMS messages, 13 mentioned polling stations which were not covered by our accredited observers.

However, some significant problems were noted in other polling stations. These fall into the categories of IEBC irregularities, inappropriate agent behavior, and bribery.

AGLI/FCPT began encountering problems with IEBC performance during the issuance of observer badges. Our CIC Coordinator, Peter Serete, made five different trips from Kakamega to Nairobi to pick them up before they were completed. Then six were spoiled and over 20 had mismatched names and photos that IEBC did not have time to correct. Seven observers encountered hostility or were refused access in eight different polling stations. Three were not allowed entry at four different stations.

IEBC irregularities included the failure of electronic systems in 34 stations (41%), inappropriate agent behavior in 11 (13%) and overt bribery in six (7%).

Failure of IEBC electronic systems was pervasive. The most commonly reported causes for this failure were password issues and computer batteries that only lasted until sometime between 10 and 11:30 am, while the polls were open until five pm. Twenty-one stations observed were able to use the electronic system only part of the time. Another 10 could not use it at all. This meant that 27 percent of the stations resorted to manual registers some or all of the time. Our observers reported that some manual registers were not organized effectively causing excessive time for clerks to find voters' listings and shuffling of voters from one stream to another.

Many stations were unable to transmit the results of the presidential ballot count electronically. Observers reported 24 of 83 stations (29.3%) that did not do electronic submission. One SMS message also indicated failure of this system.

Another category of IEBC irregularities included issues affecting the secrecy of voting. In two reported instances the way booths were set up did not adequately maintain privacy. Crowds of voters (two stations) or agents (six stations) were able to observe voters as they marked ballots in the booths.

In four polling stations our observers saw IEBC clerks issue multiple ballots for the presidential race. One observer reported to the Presiding Officer that a clerk was issuing multiple presidential ballots to individual voters. The clerk was subsequently arrested and removed from the polling station. In this same station there were 23 percent more presidential votes than in the other five races, yet as far as we know, those votes were still added to the national totals.

Our observers reported inappropriate agent behavior in 11 different polling stations (15.2%). These behaviors included campaigning in the polling station, watching how voters voted, telling voters how to vote and being uncooperative. In four of these instances a Presiding Officer or other security officer stopped the offense.

While bribery has the lowest percentage of the major problems observed, it is still a significant issue in Kenyan elections. On election day we received a number of reports regarding observable bribery. Accredited observers noted eight instances of bribery taking place in the vicinity of six polling stations. Six SMS messages reported bribery in at least four communities. In fact, bribery was the most common problem submitted to the CIC during the period of campaigning.

Looking at the pervasive problems with IEBC manual and automated procedures leads us to the conclusion that fraud on a wide scale could have easily happened and most likely did. At a minimum we recommend that a thorough audit of the election process be conducted.

A scene from Mt. Elgon (*above*)

Children in Kikai, Mt.Elgon (*below*)

CHAPTER TEN
Assessment of Friends Peacemaking Work in Mount Elgon

Kathy and Joe Ossmann

Since 2008, the partnership between the African Great Lakes Initiative and the Friends Church Peace Team (FCPT/AGLI) has conducted intensive programming in the Mt. Elgon region of western Kenya. These programmes have been complemented by related programmes offered by other Quaker-based organizations. Change Agents for Peace International (CAPI) administers the Turning the Tide (TTT) programme, which is funded by the British Yearly Meetings's Quaker Peace and Social Witness. In addition to caring for those who had been victimized, the programming was intended to help the community heal and to prevent violence related to the 2013 election.

The purposes of this assessment were to:

- Determine the impact of these programmes on individuals and communities in the region, particularly in terms of personal transformation and reduction in violence and tribalism.

- Provide input to decisions about the further direction of FCPT/AGLI/CAPI/TTT programming in Mt. Elgon and other areas.

The principal assessment method was interviews with 89 individuals in six Mt. Elgon communities. These individuals had all been participants in one or more of the FCPT/AGLI/CAPI/TTT programmes. The interviews took place during the last week of March, 2013. Additional interviews were conducted with four persons who had been principal trainers and/or organizers of the programmes. The details of the interviews and a list of the persons interviewed are found in the Appendix (p. 163). All the interviews were recorded and all except one gave permission for their names and photos to be published. Although, regretfully, we could not include something here from every respondent, all their voices have been heard multiple times through the recordings and their comments informed our conclusions.

This assessment was conducted just a few weeks after the Kenyan national elections on March 4, 2013. Although there were some instances of violence on Mt. Elgon prior to the 2013 election, it was very peaceful in comparison to 2007-08. This timing allowed us to explore the relationship between the FCPT/AGLI/CAPI/TTT programmes and the greatly contrasting levels of violence during the two election periods.

Assessment Team: *(from left)* Joe and Kathy Ossmann were serving as Extended Service Volunteers with AGLI during January-April, 2013. Benter Obonyo is a Community Health Worker with Academic Model Providing Access to Health Care in Turbo. Ezra Kigondu is the Director of the Lugari Community Development Programme. Ezra and Benter are active volunteers in FCPT programmes and committed peace activists.

Mount Elgon

Mt. Elgon, an immense shield volcano, dominates the landscape of western Kenya. Rising over 14,000 feet, it straddles the border between Kenya and Uganda. Streams and rivers have eroded those slopes so that from above it appears to be a large rippling skirt that covers an area of about 1400 square miles. A patchwork of fields, some green and others black and ready for planting, hint of the black soil, some of the most fertile in East Africa. Coffee plantations dot its lower slopes, yielding a lucrative export crop. Unfortunately, local farmers realize only a small portion of the profits which are eaten up by the cost of transportation and brokers who sell the crops mostly in the market town of Chwele just outside of the mountain's perimeter. Mt. Elgon is a disturbing combination of lush productive agriculture and high levels of poverty.

Within the mountain's ripples reside a resilient people who have endured more than their fair share of hardship. The dominant ethnic group is Kalenjin, the third largest ethnicity in Kenya. The Kalenjin are a loosely allied group of tribes with linguistic ties. Mt. Elgon's tribe is Sabaot with the further divisions of Ndorobo (the indigenous people) and Soy sub-tribes. A smaller portion of the local population are Bukusu, a tribe within the Luhya ethnic group, Kenya's second largest. Additionally there are a few Teso (a small minority ethnic group within the country), other Luhya tribes, and some Kikuyu. Ethnic conflicts over land have fueled much of Mt. Elgon's violent history.

Most people derive their livelihood from small *shambas* (plots of land) where they grow cash crops such as the small red onions and plum tomatoes that form a central core for Kenyan cuisine. Maize, potatoes (both sweet and white), and greens are often seen on passing donkeys heavily-laden with bags of produce heading to market. Some residents have small businesses, usually one-room shops that sell goods or provide services such as tailoring.

The area covered by this assessment is in the lower and mid-elevations on the southern slopes of the Kenyan portion of the mountain, next to the Uganda border. Our interviews centered in six communities: Kipsigon, Kopsiro, Kubura, Kikai, Cheptais, and Chepkube, the sites where FCPT/AGLI/ CAPI/TTT programmes have been conducted. The largest town, Cheptais, has a population of approximately 4,000. They range from there to Kubura, with just a handful of families in the village proper. However, each of the communities is to some extent a hub for the dispersed farms, which are primarily small holdings.

Mount Elgon's History of Violence

The beauty of the mountain belies its violent history and, while resilient, the residents carry deep trauma as a result. There are two types of violence that can be identified, land and tribal-based, and election-related.

A common source of conflict arises over land ownership and usage. Although the Ndorobo, also known as Ogiek, are the indigenous hunter-gatherer people, they have been marginalized and continually displaced by other ethnic groups. The Soy, another clan of the Sabaots, have at various times moved into the area claiming lands, most notably when displaced from flatter arable areas of Trans Nzoia County by colonialists. After independence some Soy were resettled on the mountain by the government in various land agreements, many of which were not fully implemented. This situation was further exacerbated by the government's failure to deliver promised title deeds for those who were resettled.

Politicians in the area have proven adept at manipulating residents using promises of land, which has resulted in cycles of violence that arise every five years with the national elections. The 2007 election triggered the worst of these cycles.

The Sabaot Land Defense Force (SLDF), a Soy militia group, was formed shortly after the 2002 elections to contest land issues and intimidate voters. Some respondents said that it was formed by Fred Kapondi, a Member of Parliament (MP) candidate. The SLDF eventually resorted to widespread violence against any who opposed them, saving some of their worst tactics for Soy who refused to join or support them. They spread a reign of terror that included extortion, murder, rape, theft, and torture. Kapondi was elected in 2007 even though he was jailed at the time of voting. This was the situation in Mt. Elgon when post-election violence erupted throughout Kenya providing a climate for continued brutalization of anyone suspected of failing to vote for Kapondi. An estimated total of 600 people were killed and tens of thousands were displaced.

In March of 2008 the Kenyan army mounted an operation which brought a halt to the SLDF. Although initially welcomed by the populace, the army themselves terrorized residents and brutalized suspected members of SLDF or anyone who might have information about militia members. Thousands of men and even older male children were imprisoned and tortured or killed. None of the human rights abuses committed by either the SLDF or the army were ever effectively prosecuted.

Winston Ndima Chemokoi of Chepkube tells of his experience when the army came.

"In 2008 during army operation time, I was arrested and taken to Kapkota where the army camp was located. I was beaten and I was really injured. They thought I was militia, but it was not so. They wanted to use me to get the real perpetrator, but it didn't happen. I found that I was suffering because of another person so I didn't feel okay. That time I was going to the hospital. I could not take care of myself. I suffered psychologically. But when I got this training on HROC, I learned something about forgiveness and I was able to forgive so that life can continue. Before the workshop I didn't go to the *shamba* (farm) because of the injuries. But now I know to talk with my family and they can listen to me and I can go to the *shamba*. I realized surely if we have peace that is the most important thing." (Winston Ndiwa Chemokoi, Chepkube)

When the army killed the SLDF commander in May 2008 things began to calm down and residents began their long journeys of healing and recovery. There were rumors in early 2012 that the SLDF was regrouping. Kapondi ran for MP again for the Mt Elgon constituency in the 2013 election and lost with 31 percent of the vote. During the lead-up to the 2013 election there were eight killings reported and some house burnings. A school was also burned and there were hate leaflets distributed. On election day and after, Mt. Elgon remained calm. Compared to the experiences in 2007 and 2008 this election was blissfully peaceful.

Positive Findings

After reviewing hours of recorded interviews, our findings were overwhelmingly positive, making it clear that AGLI/FCPT/CAPI/TTT programmes have bettered the lives of individuals on Mt. Elgon and moved the culture there toward a more peaceful one. All 89 respondents who live on Mt. Elgon shared ways these programmes have improved their lives. Even those whose first exposure to Quaker programmes occurred just two months before stated that they have already received significant benefits.

The assessment team identified nine major benefits as well as three findings that project how these programmes can continue to assist the people of Mt. Elgon in the future. With so many factors affecting the conduct of the 2013 election, it is impossible to assess how much direct impact Quaker programmes had on the resulting peaceful process. Respondents, however, stated that these programmes were one of the influences. Significant beneficial results included better relationships between tribes, neighbors and family members; improved skills and knowledge; healing from psychological trauma; beneficial impacts on community life; and increased valuing of peace.

Pastor Erastus Chesondi tells why he is such an effective leader for FCPT programmes on Mt. Elgon. "Through my experience in life and these experiences in HROC I have assisted many people. Even before telling them, they know me very well. They know how I escaped everything.

"I joined FCPT during the post-election violence. It was 2009 and Getry Agizah, the FCPT Coordinator, invited me to attend HROC.

"When I went to HROC I was not the way I am now because I had experienced bad things that happened in my life to my family. I was outside of Mt. Elgon living at Kitale town where I went for rescue to save my life. I was displaced.

"I was targeted by the SLDF because I didn't join them or support them in other different ways. They were target-

ing anybody who would not support them either financial or giving information. It happened I was hijacked by the militia group. I was taken to the forest and asked many questions. Later I was released but I was told to pay a fine. I was to pay 50,000 Kenya Shillings (US$ 833). I told them to give me two weeks and I will make it. For that I was just preparing to run away. So they took me back to the IDP camp where I was staying before.

"I went to Kitale just to prepare myself. I told my wife 'I want to leave you with the children and let me first move so I will get a job.' I stayed there for one month and after that one of my friends at Kitale offered me a place to stay with my family. So I had to communicate with my wife and the children. They traveled to Kitale. They were escorted by policemen. We had also to pay them.

"Even now I have not gone back to where my house was in Mt. Elgon just beyond Kubura. I have a plot there half an acre. What I saw in those days I still remember. I don't discourage people to go back. I invite them. But myself, I know what I'm going through. My sister was killed and we have not buried her. She was hijacked the way I was hijacked. She was killed in a manner that we cannot know. We don't know where the body was thrown. Those people who were doing such things are still there. We work with them.

"HROC helped me because to me it was not easy to tell what I had been through, what I saw. I would first see if somebody's maybe around before I speak. As a human being I was also thinking 'Why can't I take revenge?' because I have my family members and they are strong like other people. Those days they were also armed like other people.

"But after going to these programmes I talked to myself and started forgiving people. It was apparent to me that revenge would make my life end soon. I have enjoyed being in HROC. It has assisted me in this process of healing. Even my best friends are those people who could be my enemies now."

Under Erastus' leadership hundreds of Mt. Elgon residents have found help in their healing journeys. An example of his peace building occurred in response to the man's assassination at home near Kipsigon in August 2012. Erastus worked with the local HROC community to assist the widow and speak with local leaders. A large HROC group attended the funeral where Erastus was invited to speak. These efforts averted the cycle of revenge which has been part of Mt. Elgon's pattern of violence.

Helen Makoe is a 40 year-old counselor, community facilitator, and business woman who lives and works in the market town of Cheptais on the southwestern slopes of Mt. Elgon. She has experienced horrors, but she has not just survived them, she has surmounted them to become a leader in her community, promoting peace and reconciliation, instead of someone who hates. She gives major credit to HROC for this transformation.

"2007 was bad because we had no civic education. During 2007 we had clashes. People killed each other. People raped women, they raped even young children. Up to now people are still suffering because of things which happened

in 2007. Some people live with HIV-positive, some live with fistula because of female genital mutilation (FGM), but now there is no FGM because of Civic Education. But during 2007 we had nothing like that. For now women are suffering from fistula because of raping, because of that FGM. Small children dropped out of school because they were raped. They were not taken to the hospital because we had no security. But when HROC came, they came with Civic Education, so now people are educated. So during 2007 surely it was bad. I'm a victim of 2007.

"Before completing our HROC workshop, I was not a person who could forgive easy. Attending the HROC class I came to realize that when I see other people, I see myself in them. Because I can understand myself and others cannot understand me. After learning about the tree of mistrust in HROC, I found it was me because I had hatred of other people. I had no love for others. After that we had the tree of trust. I learned that tree of trust, more because I learned to love each other, to work together with friends, to sit together in dialog and talk.

"After that I passed another step, that was good listening and bad listening. Because I was one person who could not sit and listen to another person. But after the HROC workshop I am now a good listener. You can express your problem and I can sit and listen to you. I can be a good listener, give them my ears and eyes to observe what you are saying. After that we went through the forgiveness topic.

"Now in my work I see myself to be an important person in the community. I was trained by other organizations and there was no change, but after HROC workshop there was big change. For now I can be invited in the Chief's meetings to talk about HROC. I can be invited by the head District Officer to talk about Johari's Window. I can be invited even in my church to talk about reconciliation and forgiveness. So HROC has brought change in my life."

Emily Sikhoya of Chepkube is an AVP facilitator, HROC healing companion, and resource person for AGLI/FCPT programmes in the Cheptais area. She also conducted voter education sessions and served as an election observer.

"When we did the trust walk at HROC it helped me know that in life there's a time when you're blind and you need a guide. In life there are so many things we undergo that make us blind. When HROC came it helped me realize that I was traumatized during the 2007 election. My brother was killed and thrown in the forest. We've never seen the grave. My sister-in-law was picked out of her home. She was pregnant and they mutilated her body and left her there in the forest where she died. That thing affected me for a long time. HROC taught me how to get out of those effects and I got out. Many of the women I counsel have trauma. I've tried to help them following what we were taught at HROC. It really helps the women."

Help with Psychological Trauma

Since AGLI brought facilitators from Rwanda and Burundi to begin HROC workshops in the Mt. Elgon area, 21 HROC workshops have been conducted on Mt. Elgon for a total of 550 participants. Additionally, a local training for 18 Healing Companions (HROC facilitators) was held. In February 2013, just before the election, these newly trained healing companions apprenticed in eight workshops preparing them for potential election-related violence.

The HROC three-day workshop has four major topics: understanding trauma, grief, positive and negative aspects of anger, and rebuilding trust. No single workshop can heal the kind of deep trauma that Mt. Elgon's people carry. However, in 79 responses respondents report significant mental health improvements that they attributed to HROC. We can conclude that HROC has started many on a healing journey and provides healing companions and follow-up events to help individuals continue healing.

"I was one who was affected during the time this place was chaotic, and even I wound up losing my brother. I lost my properties and so many other things, and I migrated to this place and went to the other side, so I lost everything. When this training came it made me glad because in my heart I had that big weight, when I saw my brother being killed. When this teaching came up I was able to grieve about it and share with other people what happened. Even now when I share about it I just feel relieved." (Francis Ruree, Chepkurkur)

"What really happened to me, I lost my father in the year 2007 because of these politics. I lost my cow, my house was burned, I also heard the gunshots, and so it caused me to have that pressure. So after attending the HROC class it has really helped me. Death is a normal event and it is something we have to pass through. So after attending this class it has really helped me, even my neighbors. The anger I had before, I don't have it." (Sylvia Tibin, Kubura)

"On my side, I had some deep thoughts concerning my life because we were left, three girls and one boy, and that was from 1992 to 2002. We had lost all of our parents and I was really crying because of my lost brother. So when he died, every moment when I was thinking about him, I remembered the way he used to assist us, and now there was no other help. On the other hand we were taught that if you have so much pain, when you are crying you are relieving yourself. And then we were given the opportunity of healing from grief. And so from that moment, I haven't had that heavy pain in me. I feel I am relieved." (Alice Nyongese, Sesik)

"My husband was killed and I saw what was done to him. I was really traumatized. My mind wanted to go away. In fact I couldn't walk along the road for fear of an accident. And when we talked about healing it really entered me. I saw the wound that I had. Recently when I attended the HROC programme I brought my mind together. I went back again and saw where my husband died. We learned about forgiveness and then I felt good. When I meet the people who killed him I can greet them." (Gentrix Nangila Simiyu, Kubura)

New Leadership Skills

Numerous respondents related that Quaker programmes enabled them to be leaders in peace and reconciliation, or helped them in their leadership roles. Two strategies mentioned were intervening early before a conflict escalates and deep listening to all sides in the conflict.

"The programme of HROC is really assisting me as the clan chairman to bring the people together and help them to forget the past and go on forward." (Stephen Kasuswa, Kubura)

"There is a neighbor that offended me. The way I approached him I used the AVP rule that I was taught, that when somebody offends you there are very much ways to tell him politely, that what has been done to me is wrong, and I don't feel good when you do this to me. For example, what happened was I leased this farm, and this same neighbor leased this farm to another person. Then we were two people who leased the same farm. When I went there to prepare the land, I saw this other person coming also, saying this is my land. So I told that person, let us call the owner of this farm, to clarify for us. When we called the neighbor we just told him what happened. I told him 'I don't feel good when you do this to a neighbor.' The farm was one acre, so we divided in two for two years. (Alex Cheptot Ndeme, Kipsigon)

Anger management

A number of respondents mentioned learning tools, most particularly at HROC workshops, that helped them manage anger. Specific skills cited included responding to angry people with calm, listening and thinking before reacting, and methods for releasing anger privately.

"Before the workshop I was the kind of person who could be angered easily by things that cannot make one even become angry. I could quarrel with somebody who did something bad to me. But after the workshop I am now a different person because I can tolerate issues if somebody is in a bad mood. I'm able now to bring that person to somebody good." (David K. Ndiwa, Kubura)

"I used to be a very arrogant woman and I was a very mean woman but after attending the HROC class now at the moment I'm not that person who used to be that much angered." (Sylvia Tibin, Kubura)

"As we progressed with our teachings we were told that if you are angry, you can cry until you are relieved, or you can sing until you are relieved, or you can sleep. And when you are awake, the anger is over. For me, when my mother died,

I had much pain because my father married another woman. I had no peace completely. When I slept I didn't have peace. We had our dad. He initially had taken all responsibility. He was like our mother. After a short period, he died. After the teachings of HROC, even if I hear something, I don't have that heavy burden because I was told that you can cry, cry until you are relieved." (Mercy Chebeni, Kikai)

Communication Skills

Skills for listening and talking more effectively were mentioned by respondents. The terms "deep listening" and the difference between "good and bad" listening were mentioned frequently. They learned how talking can help you as a person and help you interact more with others.

"If I have a problem and I go to a person, even if he'll have nothing to help me, but he will give me ear and I will explain to him, he will have helped me a lot." (Sharon Nasimiyu, Kikai)

"After attending the HROC class I came to realize that it is important to listen to other people. I as a business lady when somebody comes, if he or she needs my help, then I have to listen to him or her, even if I don't have that help, I have to respond positively. I cannot respond in a very bad way." (Violet Chemtai, Kikai)

"The difference is me alone. I was not talking to people. I was just sitting alone somewhere and keeping quiet. But after attending the HROC, it taught me about how to stay with people and talk to people. I talk with my fellow *boda-boda* (motorbike drivers). If they're having a conflict amongst themselves, I intervene and help. They leave that conflict. Sometimes they even congratulate me saying 'If you couldn't have done that, we could have fought.'" (Silvester Chemiat, Kikai)

Knowing Ourselves Better

AGLI/FCPT workshops have taught Mt. Elgon residents skills for knowing themselves better. These in turn help them to understand each other and their communities better. When we asked what was most memorable about the HROC workshop, Johari's Window was mentioned most frequently. It has four sections of things about yourself: the public side which is things others know about you and you know as well, things others know about you but you don't know, things about yourself that you know and others don't know, and things about yourself not even you knows. For traumatized people who hold many secrets inside it is life-changing to learn that those secrets are not all there is to know about yourself.

"I can call HROC a workshop of myself. Sometimes you deeply know yourself. Others know you in a different way.

The way you understand yourself is not the way others know you." (Robert Juma Omari, Kikai)

Improved Family and Neighbor Relationships

In addition to a focus on personal trauma healing, HROC also addresses the rebuilding of communities scarred by trauma. Eighty-four of the respondents told stories of how what they learned at HROC and other programmes has helped them to heal relationships within their families and neighborhoods. In fact, the personal and corporate healing seem to intertwine, each affecting the other.

Gladys Ngaira of Cheptais attended one of the HROC sessions held in February 2013. Already she is seeing significant changes in her life.

"I had that trauma even in myself because of what I saw here in 2007. People were being killed, people were being chopped, their ears were being chopped, most of them were cut. Then I was feeling that these people are not good. I could really feel that. But when we were taught then I felt that we have to forgive one another and continue with life. I've forgiven because if I keep it in my heart, it can cause problems.

"My brother's child is a total orphan. He has been staying with my parents but he has not been a good boy. He did a lot of bad things to me, but I decided to forgive him. I brought him into my house and I've taken him to school. I decided to bring him near me so I can teach him some moral things. Since he came I can say he has changed. I talked to him I told him 'I have forgiven you for what you did. I want you to stay with me like your mother and be free.' After forgiving him I can see he's just okay. He seems to have changed. But I always talk to him. He has trauma because he doesn't have parents. There's no one to take care of him. He's always disturbed. I understand because I learned about trauma at HROC.

"I've seen changes in my community from HROC like that man who was a perpetrator interacting with people. He's not afraid. Now he's free. People think it's good." (Gladys Ngaira, Cheptais)

"In our own family we are single, we don't have parents. So I'm the first born there. Our father left our home. We are polygamists and we had conflict there. All of those conflicts were facing me. In those days I felt bitter because I had no parent there. I used to have stomach ache when somebody quarreled. I didn't eat. I felt like just sleeping the whole day, the whole night. I didn't talk with anybody.

After learning HROC I know how to control them and they are responding. I gather them together; then we talk. Mostly we have a conflict concerning land issues and education. Maybe if in the family we are lacking something, we discuss, and we come up with a solution. Everybody is contented. They respect me. When anything happens in that market where I am, they run to me and want me to solve what has happened. (Helen Kitai, Kikai)

"My husband who was killed was the head of my family and I saw my children's education going bad. Recently after I attended the HROC programme I told my son we should forget about the past. 'Let's start afresh' and at this moment he is going to school. I'm staying free. Then I learned how you can talk with your family and children and bring them close. Previously the child steps outside the door you command the child rudely 'Where are you coming from?' But after undergoing the training I see the love so that you can speak to the child and it was really good." (Gentrix Nangila Simiyu, Kubura)

"At AVP when we were sharing, a cousin of mine shared a very long story that put us all in a very bad mood. Someone had stabbed him with a knife. At long last we realized that the same person who had done this was present in the meeting. So these guys ended up begging that you forgive me because what I did should have been different." (Moim Daniel Kipruto, Kopsiro)

Ripple Effects

AGLI/FCPT programmes seem to have a ripple effect. Not only are those who've attended changed, but they also cause change in others who have not attended, as reported by 35 respondents.

"One of my sisters was keeping quiet the way I used to do. The things that were hurting her were not that much troubling but when she was wronged she just kept quiet. Then it becomes worse. But I shared with her that, when you do this and this, you become relieved." (Joseph Wangalibo, Kikai)

"HROC was the first seminar in our area. So people got together so they can see what is going on. They became friends with us who went to that class. In our community we are there like advisors. If they have conflicts in their homes, they rush and come where we are for us to solve their problems." (Hellen Kitai, Kikai)

Community Groups Formed

In some areas, HROC participants have formed community groups which provide mutual support and open opportunities for improving their area. Robert Ndiwa shared that in Cheptais they've formed a farmers' group with both HROC and non-HROC members.

In Kikai David Chepkoi Naburuk told of a group called "Amani" which received a grant of three million shillings ($35,294) for an intertribal youth football league that has "helped us find how to coexist".

Also in Kikai, the HROC community has established a group called Salu Self-help Group ("Sa" for Sabaot and "Lu" for Luhya) that is currently seeking sponsors to address contamination of the local water supply.

The graduates of HROC in Kubura continue to get together to support each other and address conflicts in the community.

Increased Inter-tribal Cooperation

"Here in Mt. Elgon we had clashes, and the reason was because of the land. So there was that difference between Ndorobos and Soy. We were not on good terms because of the land. So we took the teaching to the Soy people about peace, the way you can stay with your neighbor. We were telling them that the lands we are fighting for, we cannot take them permanently. Again we moved to the Ndorobos people and shared awareness about peace. Then we brought them together. We were doing workshops to help the people who were most affected in the Soy and Ndorobos. It was a community dialog; we were teaching them about peace." (Eunice Pkania, Cheptais)

"From the TTT we were being taught what has really caused the violence in our community and we came to realize that tribalism was one of the factors that contributed ... because we divided according to our tribe, Ndorobos, Bukusus, and Sabaots." (Gladys Chemuta, Toywondet)

"The Quaker effort is bringing people together. It also helped people to understand that even though we had been apart or we had wronged one another, there is room for forgiveness. In the year 1992 we also vacated our place, almost everybody, because we Bukusus and Sabaots, we are afraid of each other. Each and every tribe sees each other as if the other was an enemy. At the moment we are together, we now respect each other, and we are like brothers and sisters. (Christopher Walmalwa, Masaek)

Reduction in Gender-based Violence

While only nine respondents reported reduction of gender-based violence, the results warrant mentioning here. Gender-based violence has been reduced on Mt. Elgon through a decrease in domestic violence.

"I used to beat up my wife, but at the moment after attending the HROC class, now I know how I can approach her." (Robert Kimai, Kubura)

"These programmes have helped me especially in my house. Initially I was handling issues not in a right way. But since these trainings I've been handling things in a non-violent manner. I can sit down with my family and we discuss issues relating to our affairs. I don't decide myself, I decide collectively with my family. It has taught me how to submit." (Fred Keneroi, Kipsigon)

"I was not in good terms with my wife. After undergoing the HROC training I used what I learned. Earlier I used to command her and now I'm polite. Now the two of us reach a consensus." (Moses K. Masai, Kubura)

Campaign against Female Genital Mutilation

TTT mounted a campaign against female genital mutilation (FGM) in the Mt. Elgon area where female circumcision was a long standing cultural practice among the Sabaot. Fifteen respondents have received TTT training and six indicated that they were resource persons for the programme. Two people in the Kopsiro area spoke to us about the campaign.

"The TTT programme gave me the skills to talk to people about female genital mutilation. That thing of FGM is no longer there. Last year was our season of cutting the girl child and nobody underwent that." (Benson Kwalia Mustuni)

"TTT has helped me so much where I have also helped the community especially here on the mountain where we had several kinds of violence that were being done. Like one, the cultural violence, FGM. This community of Sabaots have been engaging so much themselves in cultural circumcision. You see something that is cultural is not easy to remove from people. It is a process. Now through this programme of TTT has helped so much because we conducted several meetings, forums incorporating opinion leaders, women leaders, church leaders and we've talked so much about this kind of cultural violence. Since this programme was initiated in the area that rate of cultural circumcision has come down. It had affected a culture here on the mountain. Now that a girl, after undergoing the initiation, it is believed that she is a grown up person which is not true. After circumcision a girl child drops out of school, she gets married and now after she gets married at an early age her life will not be good. Now that this girl has undergone circumcision has a lot of dangers. That canal is being affected during the circumcision. Since the introduction of this programme in this community we have curbed these injustices." (Fred Keneroi, Kopsiro)

Understanding the New Constitution

The constitution ratified in 2010 introduced huge changes in Kenyan governance. Because local politicians convinced Mt. Elgon residents that it was flawed, most did not study its provisions.

AGLI/FCPT and TTT conducted extensive civic education on the mountain in 2012 to teach about the Bill of Rights and significant portions of the document. In early 2013 AGLI/FCPT conducted voter education that focused on the voting process defined in the constitution and further detailed by the Independent Electoral and Boundaries Commission. Voter education sessions were designed to prepare voters about what to expect at the polling station. Forty-four respondents felt that both civic and voter education contributed positively toward the peaceful election.

"Even during the elections people thought that here in Mt. Elgon people would go back to the violence during this election, but that never happened because now people are educated and they know what they are really doing." (Robin Masai Kimtai, Chepkube)

"This civic education has really helped people. They know where they're coming from and where they're going.

Previously they were being used because they didn't know their rights." (Emily Sikhoya, Chepkube)

"It is a big difference from the previous election. This one, people were enlightened by voter education. But what I am saying candidly is that the election that was done this year it has been very important, more than the previous one. People didn't know the importance of choosing people. They were just being forced to go and vote, vote for so-and-so. But this one has been free and fair." (Simon Saima Chemiat, Upper Kipsigon)

"We used to term the Sabaot like an enemy. We say that somebody's staying on fertile land and we Bukusu have none. After undergoing the civic education training we realized we were going in the root of darkness but now we were going in the right direction where there's light. This is the only year that we've voted peacefully after undergoing training about peaceful coexistence. We now see that all people are human beings. This time I have the freedom of movement because of peace." (Janet Khisa, Chepkube)

Joseph Wangalibo voted for the first time in the 2013 election. "When I voted I felt happy. I also felt happy that I have elected someone whom I liked. It is different from before I voted. I just used to hear people saying that so and so is good but I had not the power to say I'll vote for him; I'll elect him. Now when I voted I was happy to be a real Kenyan."

A Peaceful Campaign and Election

Amani (peace) was a word heard throughout Kenya from national media, NGOs, candidates, clergy, and government leaders, just about everyone. There was not a single person in Kenya old enough to remember that was unaware of the disastrous violence in 2008. Everyone here and many around the world prayed that the election of 2013 would be a peaceful one.

In Mt. Elgon constituency, the 2007 election occurred in the midst of on-going violence perpetrated by the SLDF. For 2013, militia groups were no longer active. This was no doubt the single biggest factor resulting in peaceful Mt. Elgon elections. AGLI/FCPT were among the many organizations actively working to prevent violence. In addition to the programmes of multiple NGOs, the Kenyan government instituted wide-sweeping changes. In the midst of these changes and the efforts of so many, AGLI/FCPT cannot claim to have been the major factor in keeping the elections peaceful on Mt. Elgon. Respondents, however, felt that AGLI/FCPT programmes did play a role in helping to make this so.

Each interview asked respondents to compare the pre-election, election and post-election periods between 2007 and 2013. The total number of responses to these questions was 243 with most respondents providing multiple answers. People were understandably euphoric about the dramatic differences: 600 dead versus eight, tens of thousands displaced versus a handful, chaotic versus orderly election process, forced versus free voting. The people we talked to were justifiably proud and joyful about experiencing the only peaceful election that has ever happened on Mt. Elgon.

There was no forced voting. "That one of 2007 we were being given a ballot paper and the candidate had been ticked. Our duty was just to put it in the ballot box. But this one, you marked it yourself." (Richard Barkacha, Cheptais)

The campaigning this time was fair and orderly. According to respondents, campaign posters weren't torn down; there was no stone throwing and no extortion.

"This campaign was a unique one because people could attend where the candidates present themselves, the people could hear their views, and say 'Let's wait for the day.' I remember one day when the three candidates met on one field. I observed something different there. Why? Because during the other elections they could not meet on one ground."(Robert Juma Omari, Kubura)

Among the respondents were 39 certified election observers, five agents, and a clerk. All of these had the opportunity to see the voting process throughout the day and the tallying process after the polls closed. They and other respondents found the procedures to be much more orderly, well-organized and predictable than in previous elections.

"There was peace inside the polling station. It was more than my expectation because it was a lot of peace." (Leonard Barasa Chengori, Kopsiro)

People interviewed felt that the presence of observers and security officers kept people from resorting to previous "wicked ways" as Mohamed Hassan of Kipsigon put it.

"This one was very calm; inside the polling room there was no noise only of paper rustling. It was very peaceful and didn't have any rigging as the previous election." (Fred N. Lopon, Cheptais)

One sad exception to the non-violent result of this election was the assassination during the pre-election period of a man who had attended a HROC workshop. We were privileged to speak with his widow, Wilbrodah Kironget. "You know my husband was shot to death. The gunman just came into our home and shot him to death. I still have that fear that those people who came for my husband might also come back for me. But after his death the HROC community group helped me; they brought me sugar; they fetched firewood for

me. They also helped me in serving the visitors. What really helped me when my husband died was the teaching that he used to come and teach us at home. It gave me that patience. It gave me the strength and I came to realize that though my husband is not there I have the hope that there's a place where I can get another help."

When we asked her for suggestions about what AGLI/ FCPT could do to ensure future peace she responded: "If you can prevent it much earlier we don't want it to be like the previous one. I almost lost my child because my son went lost for seven months. Now he is back but he is not even going to school. So it is my prayer that the peace people shall do something that will prevent that. I'm just asking for peace. Because there is nothing that is more important than life. It is my prayer that the peace people preach peace so that when you settle root causes of violence, violence will never happen again. (Wilbrodah Kironget, Emia)

Risks of Future Violence

When asked what might provoke a new round of violence, one-half (45) of the respondents said that nothing could. They believe that a combination of factors will keep the area peaceful, including the resolution of the land issues, the security presence in the area, the programmes that have been teaching peace, and simply the fact that the people remember the horror of the violent years and don't want to go back there.

"Why stay four years peacefully and then one year of the election we fight. Then when we talk to the people like that, people voted in a historical way without intimidation." (Benson Kwalia Mustuni, a Village Elder in Kopsiro)

"Initially the problem was about elections and lands, but now there is education. People were illiterate, but they are aware now." (Robert Kimai, Kubura)

"It cannot happen. Through the peace, it has educated more of the people about the peace." (Beo Alex Kusan, Cheptais)

However, the other half of the respondents believe that a return to violence is a real possibility. Almost a quarter (21) believe that the land problem is still very much alive.

"What can cause violence is land issues. The government came and subdivided land and instead of giving a person a title deed, they cheat you. They say that 'you will be given, you will be given'. You think that you are the owner of that land and another person has been given the number of that land. There are people who have suffered psychologically and there you find a person coming and killing you. You can have five acres. Then you stay on that land to realize that the Office of Land says that they're coming to subdivide and they're bringing in another person. If the government could have been subdividing this land issuing title deeds directly then nothing could be heard of in this area. These issues of land have come to bring people a lot of problems. This time around people are knowledgeable. They know that if you have a title deed you can access a loan." (Albert Sanutia, Kubura)

It may be instructive to look at the tribal breakdown of those who say that the land issue is not resolved. It was more of the Bukusu respondents (40 percent) who put themselves in this camp, compared to 26 percent of the Soy and only one percent of the Ndorobo who felt that unresolved land issues might generate future violence. Although these numbers are small, and not a scientific sample, within our group the Ndorobo feel quite satisfied with the current status of the land distribution, while a large portion of the Bukusu feel aggrieved. This may be important information for policy makers and community organizers.

The other respondents who expressed concerns about a return to violence cited a number of possible areas of grievance among the population. The largest of these was the Supreme Court case on the outcome of the presidential election, which was pending at the time of these interviews. Eight people said that the outcome of that case had the potential to incite violence. That case has now been decided in favor of the candidate who received two-thirds of the votes in the Mt. Elgon constituency, and no violence resulted.

The next most frequently mentioned possible cause of violence was poverty and/or unemployment. Seven respondents said that the extreme economic hardship in the area was a dangerous situation.

Five respondents said that political leaders could potentially launch a new round of violence. "Maybe through the leaders. I think in 2007-2008 the leaders were the ones who incited people to the violence. But now I think we are not ready to go back to it, because people now know what is good and bad. They know those leaders are just there; they are up there; they will not come to the ground and help us. So that is the reason we are not ready to go back to the violence of 2008. I, with my neighbor, as we stay there on the ground, we can help each other. But those leaders from up there cannot come and help me or my neighbor without we ourselves helping one another." (Mary Temko Kaboto, Chepkube)

Four respondents mentioned tribal differences as a potential cause of future violence. "In Bungoma County the Tesos were not elected because we are a minority. According to the Deputy Chiefs and the Chiefs, we Teso, are not wanted in this community. The Chief is of the same tribe as those people who are against us. For example, when there is a job opportunity, they just give it to one tribe alone and we are not given those opportunities. I think when you people come and you teach us more and then we go into the villages and teach our people, then we can have the changes." (Omunangori Ebenezer Omayi, Cheptais)

Conclusions of the Assessment

How much difference did the FCPT/AGLI/CAPI/TTT programmes make? It is difficult to make quantitative conclusions, but a higher turnout for both registration in November 2012 and voting in March 2013 were cited as evidence of the effect of civic and voter education sessions. Registration statistics support this perception. AGLI/FCPT conducted civic and voter education in three of the six wards in the Mt. Elgon constituency. Total registration was nine percent higher in the three wards that received this education compared to those that did not.

Respondents were asked what were the strengths of the Quaker programmes in Mt. Elgon. Many respondents spoke of how they had been touched personally and deeply by the programmes and found them to be life-changing experience for themselves and effective in supporting community-wide change.

"I have been a part of several trainings, several seminars, but HROC is a bit unique because it touches the inner part of the life of a person, so it changes. The way they train is not the same as other organizations that just train the outer person, but you can train someone in and out. Because after being healed you can now feel health." (Francis Ruree, Chepkurkur)

The programmes were seen as being proactive, not just coming in to respond to a crisis, and that they reached to the grass roots level.

"The main thing is that the programmes of the Quakers, they reach to the grass roots level, so they are targeting the people at the grass roots even if they don't have money, but the most important thing is that they are reaching the people at the grass roots." (Jackline Chepteek, Kebee)

"Another strength that you have is that you bring the message earlier before something takes place. So if you give us and as we disseminate it before that thing happens, everybody is aware." (Benson Kwalia Mustuni, Kopsiro)

A number of respondents mentioned being impressed with the expertise and abilities of the trainers, and particularly that trainers were from the local area. "The team that you are using, those people are very strong. Your team leaders—Pastor Chesondi and Pastor Keneroi and even those people who you've also trained." (Wycliffe Kirui, Kapkeke)

Respondents gave the programmes positive recognition for the commitment that has been shown to the Mt. Elgon area by returning again and again.

"You are people of integrity because you are making follow-ups because you can send a person to go and do something but you're following to see if he's doing the right thing or not. So if there's a mistake then I know from there then you will be able to assess what went right and what went wrong." (Mohamed Hassan, Kipsigon)

Respondents were asked for suggestions how the Quaker programmes might be improved and how they might build peace in their community. Overwhelmingly, the principal response was for AGLI, FCPT, and TTT to continue bringing their programmes of peace, healing, and change to the mountain. HROC and Civic Education were most frequently mentioned by name. The organizations were asked to expand to new areas on the mountain, particularly farther up. They were asked to provide programmes in greater depth; to focus on special populations such as youth, widows, perpetrators, elders, people in Internally Displaced Persons camps, leaders, family members who witnessed brutality, and people who are not able to leave their homes.

"I don't know if this programme can afford to give us a place, a place you can build for us, even for rehabilitation, changing people like a peace center. If you can have a peace center at Mt. Elgon really we can say God has seen us. So that the programme can continue, workshops, even you can come and stay there for two or three days. You can hear what people are doing and you can say that we have done something. I think it's good if you can have a center so we can keep this programme running. And also if you have a center the programmes can move very fast. For example, old women can come, old wazee (old men) can come and you can also have their mind and see what has happened. (Robert Juma Omari, Kubura)

Another recommendation for programme enhancement that received multiple mentions was for follow-up refresher training and/or support groups for people who have participated in HROC. It is clear that the respondents recognize that their new skills and the healing they have experienced are likely to fade unless they are refreshed and supported.

Five respondents suggested that some form of material support be provided to programme participants. This is most frequently expressed in terms of lunch or transportation reimbursement. These programmes generally do provide lunch for all-day sessions. Many other non-governmental organizations provide "sitting allowances" for their participants, but some of our respondents mentioned that many people go to those sessions just to receive the allowances. The Quaker organizations that are the subject of this report find that people attend their sessions because of a desire to learn, and that a sitting allowance diminishes that intrinsic motivation.

Other suggestions included working through churches, focusing on defusing tribalism, establishing an e-exchange programme among facilitators and participants, establishing women's groups for teaching peace, doing single-day workshops comparable to AVP and HROC, sponsoring an adult literacy programme, and doing programme dramas in the marketplace.

Suggestions that are beyond the reach of these Quaker programmes include providing financial assistance to the poor, establishing a rehabilitation center to counsel youth, resolving the land issues, providing family planning assistance, establishing a youth sports programme, founding a polytechnic school, requiring the government to hire locally for local projects, providing more job opportunities, and developing infrastructure such as roads, schools, and hospitals.

A Foundation that Will Never Be Eroded

"I think that the strength of these programmes is that they have built a foundation that will never be eroded in this mountain. That is the peace that they have instilled in people." This respondent, who chose to remain anonymous, speaks in a metaphor that captures the essence of the programmes and the place. The foundation is peace and it will prevail longer than the mountain itself. Many respondents shared that this realization is growing among the people of the mountain. They have been taught this lesson the hard way by experiencing extensive violence. They have also been taught this through Quaker programmes.

It is our sincere hope that this assessment serves as a useful guide to AGLI/FCPT as they transition from election-focused work into a long-range vision for peace in western Kenya. We pray that it may be a springboard to an even more peaceful and prosperous future for our brothers and sisters who live on Mt. Elgon; that it will help build on the foundation that will never be eroded.

APPENDIX
2012 Interviews

Agizah, Getry, 14 February 2012, Kakamega

Ambiah, Cornelius, 3 February 2012, Friends International Centre, Nairobi

Amwoka, Frederick, 13 February 2012, Friends Theological College, Kaimosi

Atieno, Betty, 6 February 2012, Friends International Centre, Nairobi

Bulimo, John, 2 February 2012, Friends International Centre, Nairobi

Bulimo, Simon, 13 February 2012, Friends Theological College, Kaimosi

Ganira, Agatha, 13 February 2012, Kaimosi Hospital, Kaimosi

Grace, Eden, 11 February 2012, Friends United Meeting, Kisumu

Gulavi, Irene, 13 February 2012, Kaimosi Hospital, Kaimosi

Irungu, David, 2 February 2012, Friends International Centre, Nairobi

Jiveti, Josphat Lime, 14 February 2012, Friends Theological College, Kaimosi

Kamave, Oliver, 19 February 2012, Lugari Yearly Meeting Centre at Lake Basin

Kamonya, Gladys, 8 January—10 March 2012, Lumakanda (dinner table and other conversations)

Kijedu, Kingsley, 27 February 2012, Friends Peace Centre, Lubao

Kibisu, Churchill, 2 February 2012, Friends International Centre, Nairobi

Kinaro, Malesi, 27 February 2012, Friends Peace Centre, Lubao

Kutima, Francis, 13 February 2012, Friends Theological College, Kaimosi

Mamai Makokha, Joseph, 23 January 2012, Park Villa Hotel, Webuye

Masika, Moses, 13 February 2012, Friends Theological College, Kaimosi

Masitsa, Hezron, 6 February 2012, Friends International Centre, Nairobi

Mbugua, Ann, 19 February 2012, Lugari Yearly Meeting Centre at Lake Basin

Mucherah, Hanningtone, 6 February 2012, Friends International Centre, Nairobi

Muhanji, John, 20 February 2012, Park Villa Hotel, Webuye

Musonga, Moses, 11 February 2012, Cheptulu

Obonyo, Benter, 19 February 2012, Lugari Yearly Meeting Centre at Lake Basin

Okwemba, Eunice, 25 January and 25 February 2012, Lumakanda

Onjala, Bernard, 19 February 2012, Lugari Yearly Meeting Centre at Lake Basin

Ngoya, Judith, 10 February 2012, Friends United Meeting, Kisumu

Nguyo, Wambui, 3 February 2012, Friends International Centre, Nairobi

Sasita, Wesley, 14 February 2012, Kakamega Yearly Meeting, Kakamega

Shamala, Joseph, 27 February 2012, Friends Peace Centre, Lubao

Thomas, Donald, 3 February 2012, Friends International Centre, Nairobi

Wanyonyi, Margaret, 19 February 2012, Lugari Yearly Meeting Centre at Lake Basin

Zarembka, David, 8 January—10 March 2012, Lumakanda (walks to get the newspaper, dinner table and other conversations)

2013 Mount Elgon Interviews

The interviews with Mt. Elgon residents were conducted on six consecutive days, March 25-30, 2013. The interviews were conducted in six communities by two pairs of interviewers.

Interviews followed a list of 30 questions. Not all questions were asked of every respondent because some of the questions were specialized for different categories of respondent, i.e. programme participants, programme facilitators and trainers, and public officials. But there was considerable overlap among these categories. For example, all of the public officials were also programme participants. In responding to one question, respondents often included information that effectively responded to other questions.

All interviews were recorded. Following the week of interviews, all of the recordings were listened to in their entirety. Not all the interviews were transcribed, but all responses were captured and summarized. The data was studied to derive overall themes.

In addition to the interviews with Mt. Elgon residents who were programme participants, five interviews were conducted with programme leaders, one of whom was also a Mt. Elgon resident. These interviews used somewhat impromptu expanded versions of the standard list of questions. However, the responses were processed in the same way as described above.

The interview respondents were selected by Erastus Chesondi, who is the principal FCPT mobilizer on Mt. Elgon. He scheduled approximately 15 persons in each community, chosen to balance age, gender, and tribe, and also to include some persons with community leadership roles. All of the respondents had previously participated in FCPT/AGLI/CAPI/TTT programmes, so there was no sampling of non-participants.

A total of 93 interviews were conducted, including 51 men and 42 women. All except for four of the FCPT/AGLI/CAPI/TTT leaders reside in the southwest portion of Mt. Elgon in the following areas: Chepkube (9), Cheptais (17), Kikai (16), Kipsigon (16), Kopsiro (14), Kubura (17). The youngest interviewee was 18 and the oldest 67. Forty-seven interviewees were in the 18 – 35 age group, 40 were between 36 and 45 and six were elders 56 or over.

The dominant occupation with 59 interviewees is farmer. There are 20 employed in business, nine pastors, five tailors, three teachers, three students, and nine in other occupations. Fifteen people reported more than one occupation. Tribal affiliation was Soy (50) Bukusu (15), Ndorobo (15), and other tribes (9).

All those interviewed had participated in at least one FCPT/ AGLI/CAPI/TTT programme: AVP (31), HROC (70), TTT (15), Civic Education (62), Citizen Reporter (20), Voter Education (74), Election Observing (39). Some are facilitators and/or trainers: AVP Advanced (10), HROC (11), TTT (6). In addition to FCPT/AGLI/ CAPI/TTT election observers, one interviewee was an IEBC clerk, five had been party agents, and another was an observer for another organization. Among the interviewees were ten public officials: Assistant Chief (2), Village Elder (4), Assistant Village Elder (2), Chairperson of Clan (1).

List of 2013 Mt. Elgon Interviewees			
Community: Chepkube			
Name	**Gender**	**Age**	**Tribe/Subtribe**
Winston Ndiwa Chemokoi	Male	36	Soy
Mary Temko Kabuto	Female	33	Soy
Janet Khisa	Female	31	Bukusu
Robin Masai Kimtai	Male	37	Sabaot
Delilah Cheruto Kirui	Female	28	Soy
David Lusweti Malabah	Male	39	Bukusu
Anastasia Papa	Female	36	Teso
Emily Sikhoya	Female	28	Bukusu
Carolyn Temei	Female	28	Soy
Community: Cheptais			
Name	**Gender**	**Age**	**Tribe/Subtribe**
Richard Barkacha	Male	62	Soy
Phanice Barasa	Female	43	Luhya
Helen Tate Ejakait	Female	51	Teso
Kibet Hillary	Male	23	Soy
Alfayo Kibonge	Male	37	Bukusu

Community: Cheptais (cont'd)			
Peter Naibei Kirui	Male	29	Soy
Beo Alex Kusan	Male	22	Sabaot
Fred N. Lopon	Male	49	Bukusu/Soy
Helen Markoe	Female	40	Bukusu
Metrine Musenjule	Female	25	Bukusu
Beatrice Nekesa	Female	38	Bukusu
Robert Ndiwa	Male	31	Soy
Gladys Ngaira	Female	46	Luhya - Isukha
Omunangori Ebenezer Omayi	Male	48	Teso
Eunice Pkania	Female	39	Soy
Okisai Musa Sammy	Male	40	Teso
John Wasike	Male	53	Soy

Community: Kikai			
Name	Gender	Age	Tribe/Subtribe
Mercy Chebeni	Female	26	Soy
Silvester Chemiat	Male	23	Soy
Violet Chemtai	Female	30	Soy
Christine Chepaliet	Female	28	Soy
Hellen Kitai	Female	32	Soy
Protus Chesebe Masai	Male	31	Soy
Rev. Bramwell Moikut	Male	58	Soy
David Chepkoi Naburuk	Male	32	Soy
Sharon Nasimiyu	Female	25	Bukusu
Alice Nyongese	Female	49	Bukusu
Maurice Wangila Timbiti	Male	45	Bukusu
Silas Rotich Tirop	Male	28	Bukusu
Lina Nekesa Wakhungu	Female	35	Bukusu
Christopher Wamalwa	Male	40	Bukusu
Jusdine Wambwele	Female	35	Bukusu
Joseph Wangalibo	Male	20	Luhya

Community: Kipsigon			
Name	**Gender**	**Age**	**Tribe/Subtribe**
Anonymous			
Kipkoech Calvin	Male	18	Soy
Edith Chama	Female	29	Soy
Simon Saima Chemiat	Male	45	Soy
Emma Cheptaek	Female	25	Soy
Jackline Chepteek	Female	31	Soy
Moses Cheroben	Male	40	Soy
Rose Chesarmat	Female	39	Soy
Mohamed Hassan	Male	50	Soy
Abraham Hussein	Male	31	Soy
Wilbrodah Kironget	Female	40	Soy
Kiprotich Meng'wa	Male	23	Soy
Alex Cheptot Ndiema	Male	26	Soy
Christopher Ngeywo	Male	34	Soy
Francis Ruree	Male	40	Soy
Alfred Saekwo	Male	50	Soy

Community: Kopsiro			
Name	Gender	Age	Tribe/Subtribe
Metrine Chebet	Female	23	Soy
Milsen Chebose	Female	33	Ndorobo
Gladys Chemutai	Female	47	Soy
Lenard Barasa Chengori	Male	42	Pastor
Yonah Chepkondol	Male	23	Ndorobo
Joseline Chepkwemoi	Female	23	Ndorobo
Fred Keneroi	Male	40	Soy
Moim Daniel Kipruto	Male	26	Ogiek/Ndorobo
Wycliffe Kirui	Male	34	Soy
Benson Kwalia Mustuni	Male	37	Soy
Alex Moses Ndiwa	Male	23	Ndorobo
Benta C. Rungai	Female	45	Soy
Lilian Chemtai Samson	Female	30	Soy

Community: Kubura			
Name	Gender	Age	Tribe/Subtribe
Sylvia Cheratei	Female	42	Ndorobo
Nixon C. Chongeywo	Male	30	Ndorobo
Amos Kinja Kapanja	Male	60	Soy
Stephen Kasuswa	Male	58	Soy
Robert Kimai	Male	32	Ndorobo
Eliud Kipnusu	Male	32	Soy
Joseline Kiterie	Female	20	Soy
Kuboi Lawrence	Male	67	Ndorobo
Moses K. Masai	Male	35	Ogiek/Ndorobo
Sylvia Tibin Masus	Female	35	Ndorobo
Ann Chemtai Ndiwa	Female	40	Soy
David K. Ndiwa	Male	48	Ndorobo
Robert Juma Omari	Male	40	Soy
Albert Sanutia	Male	40	Ndorobo
Gentrix Nangila Simiyu	Female	52	Bukusu
Jackline K. Simotwo	Female	31	Ndorobo
David C. Terem	Male	51	Soy

Community: FCPT/CAPI Leaders				
Name	Gender	Age	Tribe/Subtribe	Position
Getry Agizah	Female	30	Luhya	FCPT Field Coordinator
Bernard Agona	Male	39	Luhya	TTT Field Coordinator
Erastus Chesondi	Male	40	Soy	FCPT Mt. Elgon Coordinator
Eunice Okwemba	Female	46	Luhya	FCPT Lead Facilitator
Peter Serete	Male	29	Luhya	FCPT Call-In Center Coordinator

Mt. Elgon Interview Questions

Pre-Interview:

- Introductions

- Explain purpose of interview

- Tell about recording and ask permission

- Tell about translation option and agree on language

Demographics for All Interviewees:

- Name_____
  Age_____

- Area of residence_____
  Occupation_____

- Tribe: Ndorobo___ Soy___ Bukusu___
  Other_____

- Permission to use name: Yes/No
  Permission to use photo: Yes/No

- Recording Folder:
  Message #:

A-1) In the past several years, FCPT and other Quaker
      organizations have conducted a number of programs and
      activities in this area. Which of these programs or activities have
      you participated in, led or heard about?

Program/Activity/Level

Participant/Attender   Facilitator/Trainer/Resource Person/Healing
  Companion/Heard About

AVP: Basic___   Advanced___   T4F___

HROC: Workshop___ Follow up___ Community Celebration___

TTT___

SIPP (Strategic Integrated Peace Program)___

Civic Education___   Citizen Reporter___   Voter Education___

Election Observing___

A-2) Official role in community? _____

Participants of Programs/Attenders of Activities:

B-1) (If participant/attender of multiple programs/activities) Which program/activity has had the most impact on you personally?

B-2) What do you remember doing, learning, or discussing during [name of program/activity]?

B-3) What was the most important thing you learned and how have you used it?

B-4) Did [name of program/activity] meet your expectations? Did it meet the community's expectations?

B-5) (If multiple) Which program/activity has had the most impact on your community?

B-6) How has [name of program/activity] affected your community?

B-7) Did [name of program/activity] meet your expectations? Did it meet the community's expectations?

B-8) What changes have you seen in your community that are a result of [name of program/activity]?

Facilitators of Programs/Trainers of Activities:

C-1) (If facilitator/trainer of multiple programs/activities) Which program/activity has had the most impact on you personally?

C-2) (If multiple) Which program/activity has had the most impact on your community?

C-3) Have you used the [name of program] skills that you teach in your own life? How?

C-4) Share a story that you heard from your participants about how they have applied program skills.

C-5) What do you think is the single most important idea or strategy a participant takes home from a [name of program/activity] workshop/training?

C-6) Does [name of program/activity] address needs of people specific to the Mt. Elgon context?

C-7) How are these Quaker programs different from or similar to local culture?

C-8) How has [name of program/activity] affected the community?

C-9) What changes have you seen in your community that are a result of [name of program/activity]?

Civic Officials:

D-1) In what ways do [name of program/activity] and your community role conflict with each other? In what ways are they similar?

D-2) Would you encourage civic officials to attend [name of program/activity]? Why or why not?

D-3) If we observed a [name of program/activity] trained civic official and a one that was not trained, what differences might we see?

Closing Questions for All Interviewees:

E-1) Think about this election period as compared to the 2007 election. Did the community react differently this time to the violence before the election? If so, do you think the Quaker programs made a difference? How?

E-2) Was the community voting experience different this time? If so, do you think any of these programs made a difference? How?

E-3) Has there been any difference in the community during the time after the election? If so, do you think any of these programs made a difference? How?

E-4) How are Quaker programs different from or similar to other peace building programs?

E-5) What are the strengths of the Quaker programs in Mt. Elgon?

E-6) How could these programs be improved?

E-7) How can these Quaker organizations do a better job of peace building than they do now?

E-8) Do you have any other suggestions for building peace in your community?

E-9) What could provoke any violence now? What could interfere with the current peace?

E-10) Is there anything else you would like to add that we have not yet asked you about?

Post-Interview: Reconfirm permission to use name and photo

Minutes and Reports

24–27 January 2008, Kenyan National Quaker Peace Conference

> Mukwanja, Henry, "A Presentation to Quaker Church Leaders Workshop on Root Cause of Conflict in Rift Valley and Kenya"

> Lord, Mary, "Biblical Basis and Practical Application of the Friends Peace Testimony"

> Kisaka, Oliver, "A Christian Perspective on the Post-Election Violence"

> Plan of Action

> Open Letter to the Leaders and Citizens of Kenya

1 February 2008 FCPT Meeting

9 February 2008 FCPT Meeting

9 February 2008 Machewa Chief's Camp, Eric Lijodi

19 February 2008 FCPT Meeting

19 February 2008 Milembe Camp, Eric Lijodi

23 February 2008, Report from Turbo, Margaret Wanyonyi

5 March 2008 FCPT Chairman's Report

11 March 2008 FCPT Meeting

18 March 2008 Naitiri IDPs Centre, Chrispinus Sifuna

18 March 2008 Kimilili Centre, Joseph Mamai Makokha

18 March 2008 Chwele IDP Centre, Eric Lijodi

18 March 2008 Vihiga YM report on camps at Vihiga and MBale

31 March 2008 Report from 5 camps in Eldoret, Wilson Ngaira

31 March 2008 Tuloi YM report from 13 camps Nandi North and 2 centres in Nandi South

31 March 2008 Report from Malava Branch, Pamela Masitsa

16 April 2008 FCPT Meeting

21 April 2008 Reports from visits to Turbo

2 May 2008 FCPT Meeting

9 May 2008 Organizing the Counselling

15—18 May 2008 Counselling Workshop, Lubao Peace Centre

15 May 2008 Reports from visits to Turbo:

> Report from Busia Camp, Pastor Patrick Kibuli Sitati

> Bware YM report on Migori, Osingo, Bondo, and Kakrao

> Chavakaci YM report on IDPs at police stations in Vihiga, Mbale and Chavakali

18 May 2008 FCPT Meeting / Chairman's Report

31 May 2008 FCPT Meeting

11 June 2008 FCPT Meeting

16–18 October 2008 Reflecting Peace Process, Mabanga Farm Centre

8 November 2008 FCPT Meeting

23—30 November 2008 Turbo Survey/Debrief Session

13—15 January 2009 Kenya National Quaker Peace Conference

26 January 2009 FCPT Meeting

> FCPT 2008 Annual Report

> FCPT 2009 Work Plan

26 January 2010 FCPT Meeting

30—31 January 2010 FUM Board Meeting at Mabanga, Kenya

> FCPT 2009 Annual Report to FUM Board

8 February 2010 FCPT Meeting

4 March 2010 FCPT Meeting/International Conference Call

5 March 2010 FCPT Programme Subcommittee Minutes

17 March 2010 FCPT Meeting

25 March 2010 Voter Registration Observation Training

14 April 2010 FCPT Meeting

15 April 2010 Inter-denominational Meeting, Spring Park, Turbo Division

19 May 2010 FCPT Executive Committee Meeting

24 August 2010 Mediation Group formed for mediation among Friends

2 September 2010 Mediation Group Meeting

13 September 2010 Mediation Group Meeting

26 October 2010 FCPT Meeting

22 November 2010 FCPT Meeting

30 November 2010 Progress Report to the Trustees of the George Drew Grant to FCPD

21 January 2011 FCPT Report to FUM General Board Meeting

FCPT Activities April—December 2010

Workplan for 2011

15 February 2011 FCPT Meeting

8 June 2011 FCPT Meeting

19 September 2011 Planning International Peace Day – September 21st

26 January 2012 FCPT Meeting

4 February 2012 AVP Facilitators Monthly Meeting, Nairobi

7 February 2012 Nairobi Yearly Meeting Pastors Meeting, Nairobi

9 February 2012 FCPT Finance Sub-Committee Meeting, Lumakanda

2007 – 2009 Zarembka, David, *Reports from Kenya* #1 – 94. Lumakanda, Kenya: African Great Lakes Initiative.

Bibliography

African Leadership and Reconciliation Ministries, 2009. _Seeking Peace: Enhancing Peace Building in Church and Community._ Developed by a consortium of organizations, including CAPI, World Relief, and World Vision.

Armstrong, A. G., 2011. _History of Kenya._ Kindle Edition <amazon.com>.

Barbour, Hugh, 1995. _Quaker Crosscurrents: Three Hundred Years of Friends in New York Yearly Meeting._

Branch, Daniel, 2011. _Kenya: Between Hope and Despair._ New Haven, Connecticut: Yale University Press.

CDA _Confronting War: Critical Lessons for Peace Practitioners._ CDA Collaborative Learning Projects <cdainc.com>.

CDA _Reflecting on Peace Process._ CDA Collaborative Learning Projects <cdainc.com>.

DuBois, Rachel Davis and Li, Mew-Soong, 1971. _Reducing Social Tension and Conflict through the Group Conversation Method._ New York NY: Association Press.

Goffard, Christopher, 2011. _You Will See Fire: A Search for Justice in Kenya._ New York: W.W. Norton.

Heine, Bernd, and Derek Nurse, eds. 2000. _African Languages: An Introduction._ London: Cambridge University Press.

Kenya Elections 2013, Peaceful Prevention and Community Reporting Project <kenyanelections2013.org/?m=201303>

Kenya National Bureau of Statistics, 2009. _Population and Housing Census_ <knbs.or.ke/censussummary.php>.

Kimball, Herbert and Beatrice Kimball, 2002. _Go into All the World: A Centennial Celebration of Friends in East Africa._ Richmond IN: Friends United Press.

Kinyatti, Maina wa, 2008. _History of Resistance in Kenya._ Nairobi, Kenya: Mau Mau Research Centre.

Maathai, Wangari, 2008. _Unbowed: A Memoir._ New York: Anchor Books (Random House).

Meinertzhagen, R., 1957. _Kenya Diary 1902–1906._ London: Andre Deutch.

Peaceways, the newsletter of the African Great Lakes Initiative <aglifpt.org/publications/peaceways.htm>

Wrong, Michela, 2009. *It's Our Turn to Eat: The Story of a Kenyan Whistle-Blower.* New York: Harper Collins.

Zarembka, David, 2011. *A Peace of Africa: Reflections on Life in the Great Lakes Region.* Washington, DC: Madera Press.

Friends Organizations and Programmes in Kenya

Friends in Kenya

Willis Hotchkiss, a professor at the Friends Bible Institute in Cleveland, Ohio, and two of his theology students, Edgar Hole and Arthur Chilson, came to Kenya in 1902 to establish a mission. They went by ship to Mombasa and took the new British train to Kisumu in western Kenya. From there they walked until they reached Kaimosi where they were led to establish a Friends mission. Today Kaimosi has a number of Friends institutions located along Mission Road: East Africa Yearly Meeting Kaimosi, Kaimosi Hospital, Friends Theological College, and several other educational institutions.

Friends churches were established all over Kenya's Western Province, with a few in the eastern areas and in the largest city, Nairobi. Kenya has more Friends than any other country in the world. There are 17 different yearly meetings, one in Nairobi and the others in western Kenya with over 500 monthly meetings and more than 130,000 adult members. The Yearly Meetings include: Bware, Central, Chavakali, Chwele, East Africa-Kaimosi, East Africa-North, Elgon East, Elgon Lugulu, Kakamega, Lugari, Malava, Nairobi, Tongaren, Tuloi, Vihiga, and Vokoli Yearly Meeting. All of the Kenya Yearly Meetings belong to Friends United Meeting (FUM), which has their African office in Kisumu, Kenya. Most of the Yearly Meetings operate Friends schools and some also have clinics and hospitals, including approximately 500 preschools, 500 primary schools, and over 200 secondary schools.

In addition, there is a complex of interacting organizations, both Kenyan and international, that were involved in various ways in the Friends response to the post-election violence. Details on these organizations and programmes follows.

African Great Lakes Initiative

"The African Great Lakes Initiative (AGLI) was created by the Friends Peace Teams, an organization consisting of sixteen Quaker Yearly Meetings in the United States who have united to support the traditional emphasis of Quakers in promoting a more peaceful world. In April, 1998, the Friends Peace Teams realized that Quakers in the Great Lakes region of Africa, numbering almost half of the Quakers in the world, were in countries with a great deal of violence, social unrest, genocide, and civil war. Consequently in January 1999, an

177

international delegation of seven team members visited Kenya, Uganda, Rwanda, and Burundi. From this visit and subsequent discussions, the Friends Peace Teams decided to create the African Great Lakes Initiative to support peacemaking activities at the grass roots level.

"AGLI strengthens, supports, and promotes peace activities at the grass roots level in the Great Lakes region of Africa (Burundi, Congo, Kenya, Rwanda, Tanzania, and Uganda). AGLI responds to requests from local religious and non-governmental organizations that focus on conflict management, peace building, trauma healing, and reconciliation. AGLI sponsors Peace Teams composed of members from local partners and the international community." <aglifpt. org>

In 2003 AGLI began providing funds to Friends in Peace and Community Development to introduce the Alternatives to Violence (AVP) to Friends in western Kenya and the group at the Friends International Centre that later became the AVP Trust. Over the following years AVP workshops were conducted among Friends Yearly Meetings so that when the post-election violence happened, 64 Friends had already been trained and were available to volunteer for trauma healing and counselling work with Internally Displaced Persons and other traumatized people. AGLI continues to support the Friends Church Peace Team's work of peacebuilding, trauma healing, and reconciliation.

AGLI provides opportunities for international volunteers to come to the African Great Lakes region for short-term work camps or longer as "extended service volunteers". These work camps have built peace centres in several of the countries, including Lubao Friends Peace Centre and Lugari Yearly Meeting's Peace House in Kenya. To support this work, please donate to AGLI <aglifpt.org>.

Alternatives to Violence Project
"The purpose of the Alternatives to Violence Project (AVP) is to empower people to lead nonviolent lives through affirmation, respect for all, community building, cooperation, and trust. AVP/USA is an association of community-based groups and prison-based groups offering experiential workshops in personal growth and creative conflict management. The national organization provides support for the work of these local groups." <avpusa.org>

The theory for AVP was originally called the "Group Conversation Method" developed by Rachel Davis DuBois in the 1950s and

1960s. Friends of New York Yearly Meeting's Peace and Social Action Program used DuBois' method to create the Quaker Project on Community Conflict (QPCC), which came out of the 1965 Peace Institute. Lawrence Apsey and Ross Flanagan developed the program, raised funds, and opened an office. They challenged New York Yearly Meeting Friends to get out of their comfort zones and work for peace.

In 1974 Roger Whitfield, an inmate at Green Haven prison in Dutchess County, New York was developing a program to bring teenagers from New York City to the prison to show them what it would be like to be in prison. He contacted Apsey at QPCC to lead a nonviolent training workshop, which was held in March 1975. To help him facilitate, Apsey brought Bernard LaFayette, Jr., and Paul Tillquist from Gustavus Adolphus College in Minnesota to be the facilitators, along with Steven Stalonas and Peter Matusewitch of the QPCC. The workshop included instruction in nonviolent direct action, inmate discussion, role-plays of prison conflicts, and LaFayette told of his experiences with Martin Luther King, Jr., and in the 1968 Poor People's Campaign.

The workshop was such a great success that there were requests from other New York prisons for more workshops and AVP was born. It spread quickly as people realized that everyone participates in conflict which might lead to violence. It has been applied to many other situations in communities, schools, businesses, and churches in many countries around the world <avpinternational.org>.

There are three levels of AVP, basic, advanced, and training of trainers (ToT). Each involves a three-day workshop. Those who receive the ToT training are ready to apprentice as facilitators and progress to facilitators for AVP workshops. In this way the program expands to empower more and more people to lead nonviolent lives. Excellent resources are available online for initiating or strengthening AVP programmes <avpusa.org>.

Alternatives to Violence (Kenya) Trust
AVP was first brought to Kenya in 1995 at the Maturu Friends Church. A basic workshop was held, but there was no follow-up, so it did not continue. AVP was established in Kenya in 2003 when Malesi Kinaro of FCPD, Hezron Masitsa of CAPI, David Zarembka of AGLI, and Donald Thomas met together while attending a Quaker Peace Network meeting in Burundi. The AVP workshops in Nairobi were coordinated by Hezron Masitsa, Hanningtone Mucherah, and

Betty Atieno, now of CAPI. In 2010 Wambui Nguyo was hired as the Coordinator. Since 2003, 250 AVP and HROC workshops have been presented reaching as many as 3,000 people. The details of these workshops are listed on the website <avpkenya.org>.

Donald Thomas explains that the Alternatives to Violence (Kenya) Trust (AVP Trust) "was set up in 2008 and registered with the Kenya government so we would have a formal status with the government. We have eight trustees, six are Quakers, one is a Muslim, and one is an Anglican. Five are women and three are men. We like to think of the Trust as an umbrella organization. We can't claim a national mandate as we are very small, but as time goes on it might work out like that. But western Kenya has its own arrangements through FCPT and FPCD. We try to keep informed, but we are not having any particular role in western Kenya. There is enough to do in this area.

"The AVP Trust collaborates with CAPI, and holds workshops in Nairobi, northeastern Kenya, and the Rift Valley area. The AVP Trust collaborates with other church organizations, such as, Mennonites and Franciscans. We have meetings the first Saturday in every month when our facilitators come and report what they have been doing and discuss how we are progressing with the work. They are not all Quakers. AVP is not purely a Quaker activity. It is not meant to be just a Quaker activity. The facilitators are from many varied backgrounds. We have very keen and competent facilitators." (Donald Thomas, Chairman of the AVP Trust Board)

American Friends Service Committee
"The American Friends Service Committee (AFSC) is a practical expression of the faith of the Religious Society of Friends (Quakers). Committed to the principles of nonviolence and justice, it seeks in its work and witness to draw on the transforming power of love, human and divine. ...

"The AFSC was founded in 1917 by members of the Religious Society of Friends in the United States in order to provide young Quakers and other conscientious objectors to war with an opportunity to perform a service of love in wartime. In the ensuing years, the Committee has continued to serve as a channel for Quaker concerns growing out of the basic Quaker belief that "there is that of God in every man" and the basic Quaker faith that the power of love can "take away the occasion for all wars" <afsc.org>.

AFSC has their Somalia office in Nairobi. They were not directly involved in the post-election violence work in Kenya, but have supported the AVP and HROC work of the AVP Trust in northern Kenya "where there are 450,000 Somalian refugees in the Dadaab Camp, the largest refugee camp in the world" (Donald Thomas).

Change Agents for Peace International

"Change Agents for Peace International (CAPI) is an international non-governmental organization registered in Kenya in 2006, with programs in peace-building, economic empowerment and organisational strengthening in the Great Lakes Region, East Africa and Sudan. CAPI seeks to identify and strengthen "Change Agent" partners at the local and international level and to work with these partners for positive transformation of violent conflict. Support for these partners includes consulting services (i.e., organisational assessment, project design, monitoring and evaluation), advanced training of local trainers, and financial support. ... A 'change agent' is an individual or group acting as a catalyst for peace by modelling and facilitating a creative multidisciplinary transformation of violent conflict. ....

"CAPI began as the Change Agent Peace Program (CAPP), a program of Quaker Service Norway for training in conflict transformation, human rights and democracy-building, working in the Great Lakes Region of Africa since 1997. CAPP training served as 'midwife' in the birth of a number of effective organizations for peace building in Rwanda, Burundi, the Democratic Republic of Congo (DRC) and Kenya. As they grew, these organizations recognized the additional needs of institutional strengthening and economic empowerment as part of a holistic peace building program. CAPI was created to respond to these needs, facilitating the growing professionalism of local partners, while continuing to prioritize holistic peace ('shalom') as both the way and the end goal." <capi.org>

"We challenge the systematic injustices. If the people are reconciled, what happens when the leaders begin the same old campaign tactics that incite ethnic violence? We want to empower groups to challenge their leaders. They must have a focus and be clear on issues among themselves. Then they will see the leaders' behaviour as injustice and want to address it. The path is success in small issues which will empower them to address bigger ones." (Hezron Masitsa, CAPI Programs Director <capiinternational.or.ke>)

Friends Church Peace Team

Friends Church Peace Team (FCPT) was created by the Kenya National Quaker Peace Conference of 2008 as a vehicle for intensive response to the post-election violence, as described in Chapter Four, Friends Response to Election Violence.

Friends in Peace and Community Development

Friends in Peace and Community Development (FPCD) is a peace and community development organization that was registered as an NGO in 1999. Its headquarters is in Lubao, some 10 km north of Kakamega town in western Kenya. FPCD has been involved in active peace work since 1996. In 2003 FPCD received funding from the African Great Lakes Initiative to carry out AVP workshops. This was intensified during and after the post-election violence as a reconciliation tool in 2008. From April 2010 FPCD has been supported by the George Drew Estate of Britain to carry out AVP workshops targeting mainly the youth in six locations that were hot spots during the post election violence: two in Mt. Elgon, and one each in Borabu, Mogotio, Rongai, Sotik Districts.

Healing and Rebuilding Our Communities

"In September 2002, David Bucura, then General Secretary of Rwanda Yearly Meeting, asked me to bring trauma healing to Rwanda. Finally, in January 2003 AGLI held a one-month seminar in Kigali. To spearhead the training, we brought Adrien Niyongabo from Burundi and Carolyn Keys, now back in the United States after spending more than two years developing a trauma healing program in Burundi. From this training, the twenty participants developed the initial version of the three-day Healing and Rebuilding Our Communities (HROC) workshop. Then, over the next four months, the participants conducted twenty-five experimental workshops in Rwanda and the program was born.

"Adrien Niyongabo returned to Burundi to duplicate the new HROC program he had helped develop in Rwanda. There were still gaps in the program. We needed to develop the methodology to train HROC facilitators who could continue the work in their local communities. We soon began calling these individuals "healing companions." In the AVP program, on which HROC is modelled, there is a three-tier process for a person to become a facilitator. We realized that to become a HROC facilitator was much more difficult than becoming an AVP facilitator. Because of the deep emotions caused by trauma, HROC is much more complex than teaching the simpler conflict resolution skills of AVP. As a result, the HROC training that facilitators receive is two weeks long, followed by apprentice work-shops, and then an additional one-week follow-up training where the new facilitators can discuss their experiences." (David Zarembka, *Peaceways,* Fall 2011)

Quaker Peace Network—Africa

Quaker Peace Network—Africa (QPN—Africa) began in 1998 when three Quaker policy organizations, the Friends Committee on National Legislation (FCNL) in the US, the Quaker United Nations Office (QUNO), and Quaker Peace and Social Witness (QPSW) in Britain, met with a concern for international peace work. By the second meeting in 2002 the African Great Lakes Initiative (AGLI), Change Agents for Peace—International (CAPI) and the American Friends Service Committee (AFSC) had joined the network. QPN—Africa focuses on observing elections. CAPI has taken on the responsibility for administration and funding of QPN—Africa, which trained and organized election observers for the 2007 and 2013 Kenya elections. <quakersintheworld.org/quakers-in-action/243>

Quaker Peace and Social Witness

Quaker Peace and Social Witness (QPSW) is the faith in action arm of Britain Yearly Meeting, which is involved in many activities in peace work around the world, including East Africa.

QPSW works with and on behalf of the Religious Society of Friends in Britain to translate our faith into action. We work with Quakers and nonviolent activist groups to advance the understanding of active nonviolence and its use for positive social change. We offer our resources and experience to individuals and groups through train-ing workshops, consultations and publications. We work with groups to design workshops that meet your specific needs.

Diana Francis ended her keynote speech to the QPSW Spring Conference with these words:

"Our peace testimony is not a mere relic, an optional extra or some-thing uniquely difficult and separate from the rest. It is integral to our understanding of equality, the truth we hold about the inherent worth of every person and our obligation to reflect that value in our actions. It springs from the sense we have of the life and power we choose to live in and therefore the way we exercise responsibility. It is inex-tricably linked with respect for our planet, which is ravaged by war, and by our commitment to ending poverty, which war perpetuates.

All our testimonies are challenging, to us and to the world as it is, and they are desperately needed. In order not to be overwhelmed, all of us need to choose our own particular focus for informed and active witness, knowing that we are part of the whole. Doing so will require serious effort and commitment, according to our possibilities and circumstances. This is faith in practice. It is costly but deeply rewarding, being the fulfilment of our humanity." <quaker.org.uk/past-conferences>

Reflecting on Peace Process
"The Reflecting on Peace Practice Project (RPP) is an experience-based learning process that involves agencies whose programmes attempt to prevent or mitigate violent conflict. Its purpose is to analyse experience at the individual program level across a broad range of agencies and contexts. Its goal is to improve the effectiveness of international peacebuilding efforts." (*Reflecting on Peace Practice Participant Training Manual* <cdainc.com>

Turning the Tide
"Turning the Tide (TTT) is a programme of Quaker Peace and Social Witness (QPSW), administered in Kenya by Change Agents for Peace International (CAPI).

"TTT offers a comprehensive set of tools to design and deliver an effective nonviolent campaign. The methods that have been used successfully in other parts of the world are being adapted to the Kenyan context and will help to transform the angry and destructive energy that is so easily manipulated by political elites into a powerful, nonviolent force for a just peace in Kenya.

"Young people who want to make changes in their communities are learning how to speak out loudly and strongly, but without violence. Communities are finding the courage to address root causes of their conflicts, rather than only dealing with the symptoms. With persistence and continued support, local activists will succeed in making positive changes, big and small, that will contribute to a free, fair and peaceful Kenyan election in 2012." <turning-the-tide.org>

Uzima Foundation
UZIMA Foundation was established in Kenya in 1995 to empower youth "for the improvement of the quality of the lives of the youth themselves, their families and communities. This empowerment is carried out through mobilizing youth to bring them together to share a cup of tea and establish connectedness with other youth

as a means of overcoming their isolation and an existence under a blanket of helplessness and hopelessness. Youth in one area join together to form an UZIMA youth group through which most activities take place.

"UZIMA then holds discussion forums for these youth to identity the priority concerns in their lives that they think can be addressed in order to positively improve the quality of their lives as well as those of their families and communities. The first UZIMA programme was Safe and Clean Fun otherwise known as "Edutainment". This programme lends itself to initiating activities that require no funding because the youth can start off with their own resources, such as singing, poetry, dancing, drama. It then moves into sports such as football, volleyball which require some resources for purchases such as the equipment for sports/ games." <uzimafoundation.org>

About the Authors

Kathy (Byrne) and **Joe Osmann** met as undergraduates at Michigan State University in 1966 and were married the following year. Kathy earned a degree in music education, while Joe's was in political science with an emphasis in international development. Joe later earned a master's in human relations and organization develop-

ment from the University of San Francisco, while Kathy acquired a certificate in organization development from Georgetown University. Joe's career path veered sharply into adult corrections, in both the nonprofit and public sectors. After many years as a music teacher, Kathy moved into data processing, where she specialized in change management for organizations installing major computer systems. After retirement, Joe and Kathy have pursued ways of doing peace work. They became certified facilitators in the Alternatives to

Violence Project, which helped to lead them to the African Great Lakes Initiative. They served as AGLI volunteers from January through April, 2013, helping to promote peaceful, free, and fair elections. When not elsewhere in the world, they enjoy life on a small lake in southwestern Michigan.

David Zarembka graduated with a Bachelors Degree cum laude in African History from Harvard University and obtained a Masters degree in International and Development Education from the University of Pittsburgh. He has forty-nine years of involvement in the Great Lakes region as he first worked in the area in 1964 when he taught Rwandan refugees in now Tanzania. Since 1998, he has been the Coordinator of the African Great Lakes Initiative of the Friends Peace Teams, a Quaker organization that promotes peacemaking activities will local groups in the region. He currently lives in western Kenya with his wife Gladys Kamonya.

Judy Lumb was trained as a biomedical scientist (Ph.D. Medical Microbiology, Stanford University) and had an 18-year academic career at Atlanta University, which was cut short by illness. She moved to Belize and began publishing from her hammock under the name *Producciones de la Hamaca.* She publishes books and newsletters for Belize and for Quakers in the U.S., Canada, and Kenya. "I have always wanted to go to Africa, since I was a small child. The opportunity finally presented itself with two events,

the climate change summit, COP-17, in South Africa in December 2011, and the World Conference of Friends in Kenya in April 2012. In between I wanted to experience real life in Africa, so I volunteered with the African Great Lakes Initiative (AGLI). This book was my assignment."

CPSIA information can be obtained at www.ICGtesting.com
Printed in the USA
BVOW081041130713

325805BV00001B/68/P